Blackout Gang

Blackout Gang

By Christopher Peterson

ISBN# 978-0-9904516-0-0

Table of Contents

Chapter 1 *Joliet Penitentiary* ~~Stateville~~

T he large keys rested on the right side of their pressed, green Dickies pants, making a jangling noise as the two officers strolled down a long concrete and steel cellblock range. Convicts stood in order to see who was coming down the range. Joliet Penitentiary Alpha range is a two-man hold range. That means two officers, under the watchful eye of the gun tower, must escort any inmates moving to and from the range. Some of the prisoners just relaxed behind the metal bars, while others placed small mirrors through the bars in order to see the officers. As the officers passed by the 6x9 cells, the convicts mean mugged them. Other than the noise of the keys, it was completely silent on the range. This was the atmosphere of Joliet Penitentiary. Joliet Penitentiary was where the state of Illinois sent there hardest inmates to serve out their sentences. The guards ran the daily operation of the prison, but the inmates controlled the prison. The Illinois prison system is home to over fifty gangs, yet only two gangs reign supreme. There was the Blackout Gang and the Gangster Disciples.

Finally, in the middle of the range, Officer Jones, a short pudgy guard with a receding hair line and Officer Rose a thick chocolate 'sister' who turned heads throughout the prison, stopped in front of cell 220. Rose pulled the long black nightstick from her holster. She hit the metal bars three times. "Name and number, convict."

The light inside the cell was off, which was camouflaging the paint-chipped white wall with the metal toilet and sink connected to the wall, including the twin sized double bunk bolted to the left side of the wall. Paul Jonas lay on his back across the bottom bunk with his hands folded behind his head. All that could be seen of him was his size twelve Butter Scotch Timberland boots and huge beard poking in the air. At the sound of the banging, Jonas' train of thought was broken and he slowly made his way to the front of the bars. Jonas had been waiting ten years for this day.

Jonas stood at the bars erect. His athletic build terrified most, especially the Joliet guards. He did as he pleased throughout the prison. "B73825" he said in a husky voice. Officer Jones glanced at his clipboard then looked Jonas up and down "Pack your shit. Immediate release." Jonas stared blankly at the guards. "I am ready to ride," he said.

Rose snatched the radio off her hip and began speaking while staring at Jonas. "Control roll back," Rose stopped and glanced up at the cell number "Two twenty...Alpha range."

The cell door slowly slid open and Jonas' back arched. With his head held high, he stepped out of the cell. His full six foot two frame could be seen in the well-lit range. Jonas clutched a small white knitted bag, mostly of pictures, letters and legal work. Everything else had been discarded two days ago when he received the news that his case decision prison sentence had been overturned.

At the first sight of Jonas walking out of the cell, the convicts on the tier erupted in joy. They were banging on the bars and chanting as he started moving down the range. With every cell he passed, the banging got louder. One of their own was leaving the joint, the good way, not dead or because he snitched on someone, but because he fought the system to the end and won his appeal. Now he finally had his reward; freedom. Most inmates would have been all smiles as they left the filthy violent deaths that awaited those remaining in the joint, but Jonas was of a rare breed. He was the gangstas favorite gangsta. Jonas was the type of villain you rooted for in all the gangsta movies. You wanted him to succeed, by all means, despite the many flaws of his character or the people he ordered murdered. Jonas had that type of charisma about him.

"Blackout Gang for Life!" A short stocky dude yelled from behind the bars as Jonas passed his cell. He stopped and back peddled. Jonas stopped in front of the cell and closed his fist, pounding the right side of his chest, "B.O.G. or die!" Jonas yelled. Jonas moved along the range while taking in all the excitement of the men he spent the last decade of his life with. A brown skinned arm hung outside the bars. The man raised his hand when Jonas approached his cell. "Don't forget about us..." said Amir. He was an outta-towner doing three-life sentences in Joliet for the murder of two Chicago police officers.

"Never that. I spent the last ten years with you niggas and never would forget the men." Amir stared Jonas up and down then broke into a huge smile. "Be easy out there soldier and whenever you need the team up North they will be ready." said Amir. He was from Chester right outside of Philly and was the leader of the Young Gunz street gang.

Jonas nodded his head "I love you, my nigga, and I'm going to get that lawyer money right". Officer Jones motioned for Jonas to keep it moving. He strolled down the range and stopped in front of a large steel gray door. "Control pop

Alpha range sally port," Rose said through her radio. The steel door slowly opened with a loud buzzing sound and the three entered the sally port.

****

The sun beamed down on Joliet's huge parking lot. An inmate dressed in a white one piece jumpsuit with PRISONER plastered across the back in bold black letters mowed the lawn. A thirty foot wall surrounded the entire prison along with a gun tower in the middle of the prison yard. A short pudgy guard with dark shades on walked up and down the gun tower catwalk clutching a rifle. He eyed the inmate mowing the lawn intensely. Illinois Maximum Security Prison was written on a sign right underneath the gun tower, notifying all visitors that this was the big house.

Candy Blue

A cocaine white Mercedes Benz with presidential tint pulled into the parking area. The car stopped and parked close to the entrance. Oversized black Dior glasses covered the woman's face as she emerged from the Benz. Long jet black hair covered her head which gave the redbone a desirable look. Nia stood at the door for a second and got herself together. She was small up top but thick around the hips and ass. Her all black De'ron dress was snug and tight against her body as she made her way towards the entrance of the prison. Nia's white Jimmy Choo heels made a tapping sound on the pavement. She stopped at the wired gate, reached inside her Gucci bag and grabbed her ID, flashing it to the guard.

A Black Tahoe was parked eight cars down from the entrance. Two men inside studied the powerful woman strutting across the lot. "Go ahead and get some pictures of the Green eyed killa," the man said to his partner. The police nicknamed her the green eyed killa because of her sexy green eyes. He immediately leaned over and began snapping pictures of Nia. Jonas made his way through the front gate. He was fully dressed now in his signature all black T-shirt and black Roca-Wear jeans, laid over some white Jordan's. Nia stood there and savored the moment. This was her first chance to see and hug her big brother. As a known gang member she was restricted from visiting Jonas. Although disappointed by the rules, she held Jonas down through the years. The gate buzzed open and Nia began a small trot toward Jonas, he dropped his bag and the two embraced. The men inside the SUV continued to take pictures. "We missed you," Nia said while her head was smashed inside his chest. "I missed you too." Tears rolled down Nia's face. She had thought this day would never come. She had hope though, but the reality of release was slim. "Let's bounce before these people have second thoughts," Jonas said. They both laughed. Jonas snatched the bag off the ground and the two walked through the gate. Nia pointed to the Benz, "Big boy toys," Nia said and laughed. "I hear you have a few nice toys." "Yeah the block been good to me," she said with a small chuckle. They ~~entered~~ hopped in the Benz and drove off.

The Tahoe waited for a second and then began following the Benz. Jonas lay back in the plush leather seats. His brain was going a thousand directions.

"How's mom dukes?" Jonas asked

"She's holding on, but it don't look good"

He gazed out the window and dropped his head.

"I need to get out there to see her".

Since Doris fell ill, Jonas hadn't seen her. Doris was a regular on visiting days. She made sure she visited at least once a week and would keep Jonas abreast with the family business and what the streets were saying. "She called me this morning asking about you," Nia stared at the stoned face Jonas. "She was pissed because she couldn't come pick you up...you know that has been her dream for years." Jonas just nodded his head. He remained silent trying to gather his thoughts and emotions on the sweetest woman he ever truly loved. Nia adjusted the radio and Jay-Z's classic song "The city is mine" brought the two out of their sad state of mind. "The men put together a nice package for you."

"Yeah, that's what's up," he said nonchalantly.

Jonas' paper was already ~~right~~ decent. With his hands in the dope game in the joint and Nia pushing all his work on the streets, Jonas was straight. "I told you we had it covered."

"How does the team look?" Jonas asked.

"We are strong in the city," Nia said with a mischievous grin. She was running the Notorious Blackout Gang since Jonas was sent to the joint. Now with ten thousand members strong and drug spots all through the city of Chicago, B.O.G. reigned supreme.

Jonas had started the gang when he was a youngster coming up on the dangerous Englewood streets on the Southside. The Chicago Englewood area has been the murder capital for many years. Jonas saw firsthand how life treated you if you weren't in control of your own destiny. He had that natural leadership quality to him so there was no way Jonas was going to be told what to do by anyone. So he came up with his own crew, Blackout Gang, which started off as a robbery crew. And as the Blackout Gang street rep grew, so too did the gang membership. If it went down in the Englewood area on any level, it was safe to say B.O.G. had their hands in the mix. B.O.G. was either hated or loved. There was no in between with the B.O.G. .

Chapter 2

T raffic was heavy. Trucks, cars, cabs, and city buses choked the streets of Downtown Chicago. While lunch hour pedestrians packed the sidewalks, people moved in all different directions. Some trying to make it back to work, others rushed to the Bank to make a quick deposit or withdrawal and others just enjoyed the nice spring afternoon. Downtown Chicago was night and day from the rest of the city. A black Range Rover crawled up to the red light at a snail's pace with other traffic. The sun shined on the tall office building made of all glass bouncing the reflection off the Range Rover.

Inside the Range sat Angela Becton's smooth dark complexion glistening off the sun rays. She stood 5' 6" with a body like Serna. Mary J "Be Without You" blasted thru the speakers. The light turned green and Angela maneuvered the Rover through traffic. After traveling a couple of blocks she pulled over and parked in front of a non- descript office building. That's what it looked like on the outside, but on the inside it was filled with America's finest. The Drug Enforcement Agency had leased several floors of the tall building while their original home was being renovated.

She stepped out of the truck casually. At the age of thirty-five, Angela was considered a veteran on the team. She broke her bones years ago by helping take down one of Chicago's dangerous gangs known as the "Gangsta

Disciples". With her stellar performance of going undercover and the numerous convictions that were handed down from that operation, Angela was considered one of the best in her field of gang knowledge. She even had the chance to meet the President of the United States as a result of her undercover work.

Angela moved with confidence, she dressed very conservative on this particular day. In a loose black Tracy Reese pants suit and ruffled white blouse, Angela's shoe game was mean. To match the outfit, she wore Balenciaga Black Ankle strap Glove sandals with the 3" heels. She clutched a black Valextra shuttle bag as she entered the building. Several metal detectors, x-ray machines and other security measures crowded the entrance of the DEA's temporary home. Living in a post 9-11 world, the DEA stayed on high alert for any potential acts of terrorism, whether it was domestic or international.

Two armed uniformed officers inspected bags as each person stepped through the metal detector. A large sign hung further in the back upon the wall that read "Drug Enforcement Agency". Angela moved through the machine and flashed her badge to the officers. They waved her on through; she gathered her things and put an extra spring in her step to make it to the elevator. Barely making it, she pushes her way into the packed elevator. Angela, embarrassed by her rudeness gives the occupants a smile, then pulls her iPhone out of her inside pocket and began to scroll through some of her recent emails and appointments for the day.

"Hello Angie?" said a man leaning up against the wall. Angela turned quickly and smiled when she saw the familiar face

"Hey Marcus," Angela had been in such a rush, she had failed to recognize the man.

"Did you check out the game last night?" Marcus asked the dark skin beauty. The two had been friends for years and ever since he moved to the DEA's field office as a computer analyst, Marcus had his eyes on dating her. But she was a tough grab, so he studied her. Marcus found out her likes, wants and dislikes. He went into an all-out investigative mode trying to bed the sexy agent.

"Yeah, D Rose put on a show last night. This might be our year." After arriving to Chicago out of the academy, Angela followed the Bulls. Growing up in a house of basketball lovers with her father and two brothers, it was mandatory that when basketball season came around you followed the team. At that particular time in her life it was the Seattle Supersonics because that's where she was from, but since moving and being a fan of the game, she was a regular at the Chicago Bulls' games. However, only when her job permitted it.

"Miami on our heels though," Marcus said right before the elevator door slid open. The two exited. Marcus stood six-two, weighing two hundred-twenty-five pounds and he dressed conservative in a traditional black suit. He guided Angela down the row of individuals sitting behind cubicles with computers in front of them. The pecking and small conversations of some of the workers brought a little noise to the room. Marcus turned to face Angela while walking and gave her a big 'ol Magic Johnson smile that would've been the highlight of any woman's day. He started to speak but was hesitated. He had been trying for years to get her and still had a little shyness when it came to her. They made it past the cubicles, then came upon a door leading to another larger room. A black box with a scanner was poking out on the wall. Angela pulled her badge out with her facial recognition and other information on it and then swiped it through the scanner. The red light on the black box turned green then Angela and Marcus strolled through the door.

Finally gathering the courage up to ask her, Marcus said, "Hey I got two tickets." she interrupted him immediately, "Marcus, my policy hasn't changed. I don't date co-workers." After the murder of her husband, Anthony Becton; she made a vow never to date another law enforcement officer. Anthony was killed years ago in a raid on a house that was used as a crack den. Anthony was a fearless dude and on a cold winter night, he and a team of DEA agents and Chicago PD went to execute a warrant. As he entered the house, shots immediately rang out. Not having time to react, he caught two bullets to the back of the head, leaving behind a wife and a beautiful daughter. The news of Anthony's murder devastated Angela. Ever since the loss Angela had utter disgust for being a field agent. It was just too much to lose she would say so over and over again to herself, but the thought of her daughter and the benefits she got from being a DEA agent convinced her to stay on the force, at least for the time being. She did have other skills she could fall back on.

Marcus continued his efforts on trying to convince Angela and said, "I just thought you would love to go see Sade at the Regal." She was tempted; Sade was one of Angela's favorite singers.

"Thanks, but no thanks." Angela smiled and stepped away from Marcus. She continued down the room and entered a small hallway; small offices lined both sides of the hall.

Roger Freeman emerged out of his office holding a couple of papers in his hand, nearly bumping into Angela. He stopped just in the nick of time. Roger lifted his head up and said, " I been calling you all morning...We need to talk." Angela was surprised at the request. Roger was a field supervisor with the DEA. A fifteen year veteran at the agency, he dealt with strictly organized drug gangs. Roger ran the special drug task force. At forty-two and having been twice divorced, the agency was his life.

Angela rolled her eyes at the request. She hadn't been in the field in years. Her main focus was now sitting behind the computer and following the money of certain gangs for the DEA. "I just walked through the door. Give me a second to get situated!"

"It can't wait. We're about to start a meeting in the conference room. You need to be at this briefing...It concerns you."

Angela stared at Roger with contempt. "Excuse me!"

"In the conference room now! This order comes directly from the top."

Angela was confused, Roger wasn't her supervisor but he had a lot of power around the office. She couldn't figure out why she was needed. Her days in the field were over, at least she thought.

Roger took off down the hallway followed by Angela. The two walked at a fast pace. "This shit better be about some computer shit!" she mumbled to herself. They walked into a windowless conference room. The place was spacious; a long plastic table occupied the middle of the room. DEA agents sat on both sides; the crowd was mixed with men, women, blacks, whites and Hispanics. Ten sat on one side and nine sat on the other. The walls were clear of any pictures, photos, or boards. A fresh coat of white paint was the only decoration bringing any decor to the room.

Roger strolled into the room. Several conversations were being held at the same time, which caused the room to become a little noisy. At the sight of Roger entering, the noise calmed down and everybody focused on their supervisor. This was his unit; the group of nineteen people was the ones that busted their ass on the Southside of Chicago. That was Roger's section or main concern. The DEA had broken down the huge city of over two million into sections and regions. The process made it easier for them to try and control the drug flow thru the city.

Angela followed Roger inside the room. He continued to walk towards the tip of the table where a movie projector-like object sat on the table facing the wall. Angela scanned the room and took a seat in the back of the room trying to be discreet about her presence.

"Thank you all for being here...I know this is our second briefing today but it's an important one... As all of you know we have been trying to build a case against the Blackout Gang... Nia Jonas was running this gang for the last ten years while her brother Paul Jonas sat in Joliet... Our current intelligence on the group tells us that Jonas, Paul is calling all the shots...To make a long story short, he was the brains and she was the force."

Roger gazed around the room, making sure he had everybody's attention. "He was released today from prison." He nods to a man sitting at the table in the back.

"Hit those lights" He said.

Roger presses a button. A mug shot of Jonas appears on the wall. His bald head and huge beard covers a large portion of the wall. "There he is...Paul Jonas, their leader... One slick sunnuva bitch...He served ten years on a fifty year prison term before the case was overturned for prosecutorial misconduct. The crazy gung-ho prosecutor failed to turn over the evidence of payments to witnesses, along with statements by neighbors or people who actually witnessed the murder who say it wasn't him."

Roger hit a button and Nia's face appeared on the wall by herself. "The notorious Englewood neighborhood is the Blackout gang stronghold...However, they're spread throughout Chicago."

He hit another button. A map of Englewood splashed on the wall with red dots all over the map showing where the most activity was occurring. "These are the hot spots and as you can see the entire area is red with the exception of certain spots." Roger stopped and went over to the wall as he stared at the screen. He lets the scene set inside the agents' heads. Roger steps back to the table and says, "This is a large area however, Nia has been known to concentrate from sixty-six and Ashland to sixty-third and east to Racine. Her and Jonas grew up in this area...The Blackout Gang has been involved with some of the most gruesome murders and robberies, but our main focus right now is the drug aspect of the gang."

He turned and glanced at Nia's mug shot again. "Nia stood trial for a triple murder...Witness refused to testify and she walked...Motive for the murder was the theft of ten kilograms being stolen from one of her stash houses." Roger pushed the button again and there were pictures of Nia with other members of B.O.G. celebrating outside the courtroom.

"Today we begin Operation Blackout... Although we have investigated them in the past, now with their leader being released, we need to build a solid case against them and take the whole gang off the streets. Jonas entered prison with little structure to the gang and as he sat ten years, he has made B.O.G. into one of the deadliest street gangs in the country." He turned the projector off and nodded to the man to hit the lights "Any questions?"

"Are we working with Chicago P.D.?" asked a woman seated in the front.

"No!" They don't have a fucking clue." Roger shook his head in disbelief. "This is our case...Everyone press your informants as we build out a case. When either Jonas or Nia takes a shit, I want to be the first to know...Clear?"

Roger stormed off towards the door. He caught Angela's attention. "Follow me to my office." He said.

Angela glanced around the room; everybody's eyes were on the computer analyst. She looked out of place amongst the street walkers. She gathered herself and followed Roger to his office.

Angela stepped through the medium sized office, awards, pictures and memorabilia of the DEA hung on the wall. Roger's desk was cleared except for a computer and a couple of sheets of paper.

Roger moved to the desk and took a seat in his black leather chair, looking out the large office window overlooking Chicago's tall buildings in the business district.. He picked up a few pieces of paper lying on his desk. Roger gestured for Angela to take a seat she sat down and relaxed.

"Who pissed you off today?"

"Thank them back in Virginia." He shook his head. "They assigned you to my unit."

"What?"

"I went and asked for someone to go undercover and they gave me you."

Angela shook her head back and forth. "I'm not touching this shit."

"We need you to get inside of Jonas' inner circle...And you're the best or were one of the best."

Roger placed his elbows on the desk and stuck his hands under his chin. He sat there studying Angela. Was she really ready? Angela had the credentials and the heart but her undercover work was done. Ever since taking the G.D's down in the late 90's, chasing drug dealers was over for her, at least on the street level. Angela was comfortable with her desk duties. She had a set schedule and managed to even spend time with her mother and daughter now. "Why me?"

"You're the best we got...everybody remembers your successful take down of them criminals and the numerous convictions that followed...It wouldn't have happened without your successful undercover activity of infiltrating the group."

"I have a daughter to look after now."

"I'm aware of your situation Angela and it pains me to have to ask you to go back into the field." He said with a sincere tone. Roger got up out of his seat and walked over to the side of Angela. "I remember when you joined the agency...your first case was a success I didn't want you fresh out of the academy going undercover, But it was you who said, 'I can handle this.' You helped me bring down the entire gang."

"I'm not touching this Roger!"

He strolled over to his desk and pulled a drawer open. Roger grabbed a thick folder. "Read over this first, and then tell me what you think." He slid the thick file across the desk, on the folder there were big bold letters that spelled out B.O.G. . Angela grabbed the file and exited the office without saying a word to the old veteran.

Chapter 3

Nia navigated the Benz down the residential neighborhood of Hyde Park it was beautiful. The who's who of the Chicago stayed in the area. She rode in silence, so Jonas could get his head right for the up-coming visit. Nia slowed down and pulled into a long driveway. She stopped and the two exited the vehicle. They headed towards the Grande stone manor home. The place combined stately elegance and modern luxury.

"Damn, this is what I been missing huh?" Jonas asked shaking his head at Nia.

"This is the good life...It ain't like how we grew up."

A couple of people ran out of the stunning home. They raced across the perfectly trimmed grass towards Jonas. He hugged, and kissed a few of the woman. They were mainly old friends and family members of his daughter's mother, Lisa. But they all considered Jonas family no matter how much time had passed.

Ten year old, Tia stood in the doorway just staring at Jonas. She was cute and had pretty long hair; most people thought she was Nia's daughter by her close resemblance of her aunt except Tia's eyes were brown, where as Nia's were green. The little feisty girl folded her arms, upset that her father, Jonas was giving everybody else his attention. He looked over the crowd and locked eyes with the light skinned girl. She quickly turned and walked back into the house. Nia watched the silent interaction between Jonas and Tia. She just shook her head. "That girl got too much attitude." she mumbled to herself hoping Jonas didn't hear her remark.

They all walked into the house. Thick crème carpets were spread across the floor and lead all the way up the stairs leading to the four bedrooms in the home. Red suede furniture set decorated the room with matching smoked glass tables occupying the living room. On the wall was a fifty-two inch flat screen television. Jonas picture appeared on the screen as the news anchor was talking about Jonas. Tia sat on the sofa arms still folded watching the screen. "Turn that shit off." said Nia. She grabbed the remote off the table and hit the switch. Tia just stared at Nia. She was used to her aunt's evil ways and even though she loved her, the two battled each other verbally non-stop. Nia loved it. She was trying to raise her niece to be tough and not to take any bullshit from anybody, including herself.

Jonas plopped down on the seat next to Tia. It had been awhile since the two had seen each other. Her mother, Lisa had been against her daughter visiting prisons no matter who was there. Nia protested but Jonas understood her reasons so he didn't challenge Lisa on the issue. He wanted a better life for Tia; He didn't want her to accept the fact that prison was a common place that most of her male friends would end up at.

He picked her up off the couch and sat the little girl on his lap. Jonas closed his eyes and kissed her forehead.

"You grew up to be so beautiful."

Tia smiled. "Thank you daddy."

"Wow, you've grown up so fast." He said.

"Yeah, but she got your stubborn ways." Lisa said walking down the steps.

The petite woman smiled at her high school sweetheart. Her deep dimples and short hairstyle gave the woman an exotic look. She sashayed towards the couch by Jonas. He acted as if she didn't exist Lisa stood there in front of him wanting to be noticed. Jonas gave up on the sexy yellow bone a long time ago. She had committed a grave sin that had almost cost her, her life. Jonas let it slide, but always kept the betrayal in his memory bank. Lisa was a hairstylist by day, she owned an exclusive hair salon in the city of Chicago, but Jonas still took care of her from the joint even though she was no good he helped her for the sake of Tia.

"Paul, we need to talk when you get a minute."

Jonas kissed Tia on the cheek, "Aight." he raised Tia off his lap and got up. Lisa guided him into the kitchen.

"Lisa, I'm proud of you."

"Thank you, but it's not easy." Lisa said and strolled across the white tiled floor.

A medium size stainless steel refrigerator was surrounded by wooden cabinets, painted white. She reached in the refrigerator and grabbed a water bottle.

"What's on your mind?"

"Paul your daughter needs you...I hope you spend more time with her than trying to be some damn hood star."

"Save the bullshit speech!"

Lisa slammed the bottle on the counter making a little noise. "Bullshit speech! Nigga, you got some damn nerve. You haven't been in your child's life for the last ten years... The hell with this house you bought or the other countless things you've done...She needs a father in her life!"

Jonas glances around the kitchen.

"Motherfucka, be a real father!" said Lisa.

She was angry at this point, she really didn't mean the words, but her emotions spoke. She was mad at the fact that Jonas didn't want her no more. Lisa begged, pleaded and apologized countless times for her vicious violation of having a relationship with one of Jonas's friends. Jonas had understood that fifty years was a long time for anybody to wait, but he couldn't grasp the fact that she had sex with one of his friends.

Jonas grabbed her around the neck with one hand and slammed her against the refrigerator. He slapped Lisa with his free hand.

"Bitch I made you! Don't ever forget that!" He went to raise his hand again for another slap, but he stopped short and just pushed his index finger on the side of Lisa's head. "Don't ever talk to me like that again... You're lucky I don't bury your stupid ass for all the bullshit you been on!"

A tear rolled down her cheek, which brought Jonas out of his trance. He released the clutch on her neck. She coughed and tried to maintain her breathing.

"Get out of my house! Get out!" she screamed.

"TiaTia's coming with me."

"Paul, you're not taking my baby nowhere."

Lisa ran out of the kitchen, she slightly bumps Nia stepping into the kitchen. Nia stood there with a confused look on her face.

"We out!" said Jonas.

Nia shook her head and followed Jonas out of the kitchen. He stopped in the living room and kissed Tia.

"I love you... Daddy be back for you later."

Jonas said his goodbyes to everybody else and was out of the door.

Chapter 4

Angela moved through the living room, her tenth floor two bedroom condo was nicely furnished with family pictures on the walls, a fluffy crème and tan sofa set and polished wooden table set surrounding the room and a forty-inch plasma television set was mounted to the wall.

Nikki Becton sat in the middle of the living room playing with her baby dolls. The six year old was a shorter version of her mother except her hair wasn't as long. Angela watched her for a couple of hours as she played quietly by herself, Nikki was her life. Angela's everything. She thought hard over the last few hours about going undercover again. She was stuck between a rock and a hard bottom. The agency had authorized her to go she couldn't just tell them no. This was the job she signed up for but the game changed so drastically since her ties on the streets. The players were different. Murder was an accepted practice of the trade now. Unlike it was when she was a field hound, Angela second-guessed herself over and over again. But it all came down to the same result. It was her duty to protect the citizens of America. This was the oath she'd sworn when she became a member of America's Drug Agency.

"Nikki, go get your stuff. We are going to see granny."

She ran off towards her room, Nikki was exited to go see granny. She loved those fresh apple pies that granny made every time she stayed with her. Angela snatched the phone off of the table and dialed a number, "Momma, we are headed your way...I need you to look after Nikki for a little bit...Hopefully it won't be long I love you so much, thanks." She hung up the phone and started towards Nikki's room.

Angela stood in the doorway as Nikki stuffed her clothes into her pink luggage bag. Nikki was used to going to granny's house for a couple weeks when Angela had to make runs out of town for the agency.

"Did you make sure you packed panties this time?" she asked smiling at the beautiful little girl.

"Yes mommy."

Angela stepped off and walked to her room. A queen size bed with a fluffy comforter and four big pillows occupied the corner of the roomright next to the window. She raised her curtains and a beautiful view of Lakeshore Drive greeted her. Angela strodeto the closet,and she began to undress and took off her expensive black pants suit slowly. Angela still haddoubts about the mission. The more she tried to block them out, the more Anthony popped up in her head. He would've advised her against it. Anthony hated the fact that she went undercover. Anything could go wrong! He used to tell her.

Angela slipped on a pair of sweatpants, and a sweat shirt. She reached up on top of the shelf in the closet and grabbed her Glock Nine millimeter. Angela placed the weapon on the nightstand.

Nikki stood in the door holding her case and watched her mother's every move. "I'm ready mommy." Angela smiled at the happy kid. 'Damn, you look just like your daddy.'

Angela thought to herself. She strolled over to Nikki and picked her up, giving her a soft kiss on the lips. Nikki quickly wiped her mouth with the back of her hands.

"Don't wipe my sugar off," said Angela amused

She kissed Nikki again and put her down.

Chapter 5

The line grew by the minute to get into the exclusive party of the Blackout Gang. The fifty yard line was the place to be on this Saturday night. Anxious party goers were dressed in all black attire from their shoes to their expensive ladies' handbags. The color for the night was black, a black carpet with small pillars ran from the sidewalk towards the entrance of the club. Five huge men, wearing black jeans and black t-shirts with security on the back in white lettering managed the crowd of people trying to get access to the club. A black Maserati pulled up to the curb. Jonas exited the vehicle by himself. He was draped in a black Prada suit with a pair of black Salvatore Ferragamo shoes. Jonas held a phone to his ear.

"Welcome home, Jonas!" A female yelled from the crowd. Jonas just smirked and waved at the sexy lady. Two of the security guards rushed over to escort Jonas into the club. A large banner underneath of the fifty yard line logo read, "BLACKOUT AFFAIR" in white. They hurried Jonas into the building while a short man in a red t-shirt went and got behind the Maserati in order to park the car in the valet section. Less than a minute later a black on black Rolls Royce Ghost pulled up in front of the club. Nia exited the vehicle dressed in a black Alexander McQueen lace dress with a pair of Christian Loubtins, and clutched a Michael Kors handbag. A devilishly beatiful woman leaned out of the passenger side and climbed out of the car. Trina was also dressed in black; she had on a skin tight Gucci dress with a pair of Gucci heels that matched her dress to the tee. Two other females hopped out the back seat of the Rolls. Nia's squad was looking stunning. Men and women wolf whistled and hollered and said little sexual things, as the four women were escorted into the club.

Biggie's, "Sky is the limit" blasted through the semi-dark club. The club was packed and yet it l was still early in the night. Nia had planned Jonas's coming home party well. She invited the whole city out for the event. Two large steel cages hung from the ceiling, both were situated on the left and right side of the small stage. An exotic looking woman with just body paint on designed to mimic a bikini swim suit, danced seductively on the left side. While, another chocolate girl with just a bikini on and no top dropped it like it was hot.

Nia's crew strolled through the crowded dance floor, nodding their heads to the music. Nia stopped occasionally and hugged friends and associates, then she headed up to the V.I.P. section with her crew. Jonas lounged back on the couch, as he puffed on a cigar. Two bottles of Ace of Spades were in a bucket sitting on ice, lying on the black table begging to be opened.

Fifty yard line's V.I.P. section was rich; the section was on the second tier and was sectioned off by security guards. It was an open section, so that from VIP you could still view the dance floor downstairs. A couple of B.O.G.'s soldiers, and other members where lounging around the spacious VIP section with some of the toughest chicks in the GO. B.O.G. owned the night.

Nia and her crew moved past the bodyguards. She was carrying a large handbag. Nia entered the spot and tossed the bag on the table. It landed right next to the bottles of liquor. Jonas stood up from his seat, he kissed Nia on the cheek, then went through the bag. Several stacks of hundred's were stacked snuggly in the bag.

"How much is this?" Jonas whispered in Nia's ear.

"Three hundred!" She responded back in his ear, trying to make sure he heard her right over the loud noise of the club.

Young Tayda stepped on the stage. The fly spitting rapper from Englewood hugged the mic tight and said "What's good Chi-town?" The crowd went wild. Young Tayda was well-known throughout the "Go." He had been tearing up the mix tape circuit for years. Now, with his new distribution deal with Street Dreamz Entertainment, Young Tayda was pushing his independent label "Ward Life'" through the roof. Tayda was covering a lot of ground in America's urban neighbor-hoods.

Young Tayda waved the crowd to settle down, and screamed through the mic. "BLACCCK OUUUT GANG!" He hollered stretching out his words for the crowd to hear. The crowd went crazy and started yelling "B.O.G.! B.O.G.! B.O.G.! B.O.G.! B.O.G.!"

"Okay yeah! This dedicated to the big homie Jonas... Welcome home gangsta... B.O.G. FOR LIFE!"

The spot light shined on Jonas. He raised his hand holding a bottle of Spades, in order to acknowledge Young Tayda's remarks. After the show of appreciation Young

Tayda went straight into freestyle. The crowd was bobbing their heads, and was mesmerized by his flow.

Jonas turned around to his crew; he motioned for them to follow him. The twelve men and four females got up and trailed behind Jonas. He went down on the first level and strolled over by the stages exit sign, right underneath of the exotic woman dancing to Young Tayda' song. They entered a hallway with three doors on the right side of it. Nia sped up to the front. "Ay, the second door is ours." She went into her purse and pulled a key out.

Nia unlocked the door and entered the room. Everybody followed her lead.

Nia had discussed the idea with Jonas of the crew having an emergency meeting. Jonas thought it was a good idea, but he refused to have any meetings in Chicago, especially in the day time. He did some long and hard thinking in prison about coming home and walking into an indictment. Jonas had refused to go out like that. So many legends in Chicago fell that way. He thought to himself on numerous occasions. He had planned to be discreet a little, with his gang's business. The flashy cars, homes and expensive clothes, he could account for. Nia had established a lucrative real estate business with her childhood love that couldn't be penetrated by the Feds. It was perfectly legit.

With Jonas's worries of the crew's top members meeting in the day time, Nia figured that Jonas's party would be a good opportunity for everybody to meet and get on the same page. A wet bar sat in the corner of the room with a long conference table in the middle. Everybody took seats around the table. Jonas walked to the front of the table; He took a couple puffs of his cigar. Jonas waited for a second and blew the smoke out. "Thank y'all for coming out tonight for my party...I know it's been a week and I haven't even seen some of you yet, but it's all love."

The crowd of people just nodded slowly at him. "Truly it's an honor to be amongst y'all again and have our team even stronger."

He puffed the cigar again and dropped his head in deep thought, then raised his head again to speak. "While upstate I did some thinking about our direction and established a few alliances with a couple other leaders of the different gangs... and decided what type of role we must play throughout the "GO." He stopped to scan the room and all eyes were still on him. "Diamond Dre, you lockdown the low end... everything from fifty-first and State to the Ickes." Jonas said, glaring at the man wearing a tailor made black and dark purple Barbara Bates suit.

"What about Ida B. Wells?" asked Dre.

"That's your area, so lock it down soldier." Diamond Dre nods his head in approval from Jonas's remark. "Black Smoke, What's good fam?"

"Chasing a dollar," the charcoaled color man said, sitting next to Nia.

"Sorry to hear about your brother." Jonas shook his head in disbelief.

Ready-Rock, Black smoke's brother, was killed in cold blood. He had robbed a bank out in Gary, Indiana with a couple Mafia Insanes that he had met in the joint. The group came off with five hundred thousand by hitting the bank in the morning and gaining access to the volt. With a smooth getaway, Reddy-Rock and the two Mafia Insane gang members fled to Chicago. They ended up in a house on the Westside. It was one of the Reddy-Rock's girls spot. The crew set up shot and gathered at the table counting the money. Reddy-Rock's friend, Shyra seen all the money spread out on the table and secretly counted the one to herself. She had seen the stacks of money, a thousand covering today. Shyra then called her brother, Ice who was a member of the four corner hustler gang. Ice got a couple of soldiers together and they ran in Shyra's house. The access spot was easily accessible, she had left the front door unlocked and went upstairs in the room to avoid getting killed. The crew stormed the crib, they caught Ready-Rock off guard along with his two Mafia Insane partners. Ice rounded them up in the dining room while his partners gathered the money up on the table. Ice shot all three of them in the back of the head then fled the house. Shyra was left to deal with the aftermath. She stood firm, and convinced the police it was a robbery that ended in murder, if it wasn't for her hiding upstairs under the bed she would have been killed too.

Black Smoke got the news of Ready-Rock's death on a Friday night. Word was passed around of Shyra's role in the incident. Smoke and a couple of B.O.G.'s soldiers snatched Shyra up and tortured her. She gave up everybody's role in Ready- Rock's murder. Shyra still wasn't spared from her assistance with solving the murder. They sliced Shyra's throat and waited until late at night to hang Shyra by her ankles, attached to a tree for the whole Westside to see. B.O.G. was making a statement. That was word on the streets ever since her murder, Black Smoke been on Ice's heels trying to find him and the other participants in Ready-Rock's murder.

Jonas was well aware of the incident. Doris had fully explained the story to him while on a visit in Joliet one day. "This is the life we choose, big homie!" Black Smoke said, trying to block out the image of Ready-Rock lying in a casket.

"Nia put together a nice care package for lil Rock... I know he straight, but this one is from the team."

"It's done!"

"Smoke you lockdown the North side...Keep ya foot on those niggas neck in the greens," said Jonas.

"Those Latin Kings got strong up there."

"I know, but I reached out to a couple of folks while I was upstate...I made an alliance... "we supply the work to them and in return we get a couple of their money making corners. Nia is going to give you a name and number to get in contact with my man up there and everything is going to run smooth."

"It's Pablo right!" asked Black Smoke.

"Yeah!"

"I'll speak with him then."

"Flip Toney, what the Westside look like?" asked Jonas.

Flip sat back smoking a Newport. His long dreads and brown skin complexion would've made you think he was from the islands, but he wasn't. Flip Toney was a Westside G. He had been recruited by Nia when Jonas got her access to an out-town connect. Flip was 6"2 and two hundred and fifty pounds. The black linen suit barely t hid his massive, athletic frame underneath.

"The soldiers are strong and ready." Flip said.

Jonas stood there and glanced over his members. He had a plan and he hoped it panned out. Chicago would be B.O.G.'s, not one group ever fully controlled the city. Throughout the long history of Chicago's gang life and organized crime existence, the crews always battled for supremacy. The only gang that ever came close to the full control was the G.D.'s, who also failed due to the numerous convictions of key members who had the brains and visions to take the group to the next level.

After Nia had caught the triple homicide, Jonas put Ken-Ken in charge of handling the work. B.O.G. had acquired a major connection from Vancouver named Marc Anthony. He supplied Nia at first with kilograms of china white, (heroin) and kilos of cocaine. Jonas got introduced to the man through his partner Whitey, who stayed in Washington D.C. moving heroin on America's dangerous streets.

Whitey had gotten arrested coming through Illinois with a million dollars in cash inside the trunk of his car. He hired one of the top guns in Chicago to represent him in the State's court system. Whitey's lawyers made some moves and worked some back door favors. The state kept the case and didn't notify the IRS or the federal authorities. In return, the money was released to Illinois's treasury department. Whitey was then sentenced to two years in the states penitentiary at Juliet where he met Jonas. He helped Whitey throughout his time. By taking him under his wing and giving him B.O.G.'s protection in the joint. Whitey was grateful for this act; it wasn't that Whitey was a sucker, he just was an out of Towner with money, and was a huge target for the numerous gang members running crazy around Joliet. In return for his favor, Whitey introduced him to Marc Anthony, originally from Spain, but living in Canada. Marc was Spanish and black mixed. His Spanish features were the most dominant. He blessed Jonas with all the drugs that his crew could handle.

Jonas glanced at Ken- Ken. "How's my man Marc Anthony?"

"I spoke with Marc today...He sends his love and wants you to get with him immediately after you settle in a bit," said Ken Ken.

Ken -Ken was Jonas childhood partner. They both came up in Englewood together. Where Jonas liked to fight, Ken Ken liked to sell drugs. He had started at the tender age of eleven serving nickel bags of weed in yellow envelopes. Ken- Ken's older brother, Pike had him on the block pushing the product. Pike instilled a hustler's mentality in the young kid and Ken- Ken took it and ran. Jonas loved that about him, Ken Ken was a real go-getter.

He slouched back in the chair, Ken- Ken wore a suit by Louis Vuitton. It was black with white pen stripes. Ken's shiny bald head always had people saying that he resembled 2pac.

Ken controlled the Southside, but supplied the other members also. He even had some clients on the side that Nia and the other board members didn't know about.

"Ken hold that Southside down!" said Jonas.

"You already know!"

"Keep ya foot on those C-notes necks." Nia said, trying to throw a shot at Ken -Ken.

The C-notes had been making a lot of news lately. Murdering, robbing and taking over a couple of off brand gangs corners. Chicken G, who was their leader, was making a statement in Chicago; but Nia refused to let them gain any type of rep off of B..O.G.

Chapter 6

J onas had gone over a couple more pressing issues with the group and then everybody returned back to the party. It was just after two o'clock and everybody in the club was either drunk or high. Girls danced half-naked on the floor while the men played them close, trying to set up their one nighters' for the night. Nia strolled through the dance floor and hit the bar. She grabbed a bottle of Moet and raised it up to salute Jonas. He smiled and nodded his head at her.

Jonas gazed at the crowd. He wasn't looking for anybody in particular, but spotted a familiar face. Bobby Mackey was barging his way through the party goers along with three of his goons.

Bobby was the leader of a gang called the Bogus Boyz. They were a group first organized by the G.D. to take care of some dirty work, but shit got out of hand. They started murdering innocent people and killing police officers that were on the take for no apparent reason. So the Gangsta Disciples disowned them and took them to war. The beef had gone on for a couple of years with both sides both losing soldiers. That's when the old man, Larry Hoover gave the order to a cease fire and just like that, both sides stopped. The old man made the order on the strength that Bobby was somehow related to him down the line. But, ever since the G.D.'s let them breath, Bobby Mackey turned it up on the rest of Chicago. His claim to fame, after the cease fire was how he extorted Rico; a major heroin dealer from East St. Louis, Rico had stopped the payments to the Bogus Boyz. Bobby got offended. So, Bobby and a couple of his goons grabbed Rico coming out of a club. They kidnapped him, took all his money and then killed him. Bobby had personally cut Rico's head off with a chainsaw and set it on the doorstep of Rico's baby's mother, for her to find in the morning before she took the kids to school.

Bobby was a short man; he stood five-one and weighed a hundred and fifty pounds. Bobby and his goon's were not dressed in suits, they all wore black jeans and black t-shirts. He pushed a female dancing by him up against a tall, dark skinned brother sipping on a drink. Bobby seen the drink spill on his clothes, he gave the man a dangerous glare with his piercing brown eyes. The man dropped his head and tried to wipe off his shirt. Jonas saw the whole scene play out from the top deck of the VIP section. He knew Bobby was always on some bull crap.

"Blackout Crew brought the bar...Free drinks at the bar!" The DJ screamed through the mic.

A swarm of females headed to the bar trying to hurry up and get their last drinks in before the club closed. Bobby made his way to the VIP area. He stopped at the sight of the security guards. They looked back at Jonas to confirm if it was alright to let Bobby and his crew through. Jonas nodded to them that it was okay. Bobby moved past the two husky, football playing looking guards. He wasn't intimidated by their size, not because he was the coldest killer in the streets, but because he had a short man complex. Bobby thought that everybody always was trying to play him because he was short. That's what made him such a dangerous person to deal with. He headed up the steps to meet Jonas. Bobby grinned at the big man and stuck his hand out; they shook hands and embraced each other. The two had a little history together.

They weren't the best of friends but they were not enemies either, at least not yet.

"Welcome home soldier." Bobby said, while his goons stood behind.

"Thanks! What brings you out tonight? I know the party scene is really not your type of event." said Jonas. He was trying to be diplomatic, while also trying to figure out what Bobby was up to.

"Nah, I just had to come down and see my old friend in person myself."

"Nia reached out to you yet?" Jonas was curious if this was the reason for his aggressive behavior tonight.

Nia and a couple of soldiers had gone over to pay Bobby a visit at Murders Row. The place was a major heroin spot that Bobby ran with his brother, Omar. Nia had went over and asked him to join the new organization that Jonas was trying to put together. Bobby declined and had even threatened the B.O.G. with war if they ever tried to disrespect him again like that.

Bobby eyed Jonas. "Word throughout the 'Go' is that you're trying to stake claim to the city...On some get down or lay down shit."

Jonas smiled and said, "Come on Bobby...Never that...I could never pull off any shit like that without ya help." Jonas tried to stroke his ego.

He didn't want to go to war with the Bogus Boyz. Jonas just wanted them to be represented at the table or else they were history. It wouldn't be Jonas's call unless the Board members authorized it.

"I'm just trying to bring a little structure to the city, that's all."

"Damn, so you sent ya crazy ass sister to me...You know the Bogus Boyz always did our own thing." Bobby said, still upset.

The Bogus Boyz did do their own thing, but was loosely organized and with that simple fact, some of their members didn't always follow Bobby's orders. Even though he took them to war for that, it still was a major flaw to them as a gang.

"Listen no disrespect to you, but the Bogus Boyz are not even relevant in the 'Go'." Jonas had lost his cool.

When Bobby mentioned Nia, Jonas remembered the disrespect he had showed her. Nia wanted to go back and kill him that night but Jonas wanted to play it cool. Business being conducted was more important than Bobby saying some disrespectful things out of his own stupidity.

"Not relevant!"

"You see, structure determines the function and most groups fail because they adopt a function determined structure policy...Y'all lack structure."

"What the fuck are you talking about??? Jonas that ten years fucked ya head up!" Bobby said.

"I take it that went over ya head."

Bobby was frustrated with Jonas talking him and his gang down. He had already determined that B.O.G. was going to be a problem, but thought that since Jonas came home, things would be different. He leaned forward in order to get a little closer to Jonas. Throughout the heated conversation, Black Smoke had walked up to Jonas's side to see what was going on. Bobby tried to get a little bit closer in order to smack Jonas. Smoke gave him a hard stiff arm to the chest. With Bobby being so light he fell into his goons almost hitting the floor, if it wasn't for them catching him. Bobby quickly made it to his feet again; he had murder in his eyes. "Ay, you bitch ass nigga...I'm going to bury ya punk ass."

Ken- Ken ran over and got in the middle of the two. Jonas whole crew stepped forward. Bobby saw he was outnumbered. He turned and tapped his three men to move, they made their way down to the dance floor. Nia half-drunk didn't notice the commotion at first. She caught the end of it, when Smoke had pushed Bobby. At first she was going to race to the VIP section, but decided on a better strategy. She called Bolo over and whispered in his ear.

Bolo had been a hitter for the crew for years. He caught Bobby's attention. He twisted his face at Bolo. Bobby wanted all of the crew dead now.

"I should've done killed that nigga years ago." Bobby mumbled to himself.

They made their way of the club. Bobby had enough of B.O.G.'s shit, now was the time.

Two of the B.O.G.'s soldiers trotted over to Bolo by the bar and Bolo nodded for them to follow him. They followed Bobby from a distance.

A blue Navigator sped up to the entrance of the club. One of the valet workers exited the jeep. Bobby stormed straight for the passenger seat.

"Get behind the wheel!" he ordered one of his goons.

The other two got in the back of the SUV. They sped off as Bolo stepped out of the club.

The Navigator circled the club twice then pulled over around the corner.

Bobby was going off inside the SUV. The two goons in the back seat were loading their AK-47 assault

rifles.

"Hand me one of those!"

The goon behind the driver did as he was told. "Go ahead and pull off...We going to catch them on the let out."

As soon as they pulled off, a dodge caravan pulled alongside of the Navigator. Bolo stuck his AR-15 out of the passenger side window.

"Oh shit! GO! GO!" Bobby screamed seeing the automatic barrel out of the window. From the position he was in he couldn't get a clear shot.

Bolo started firing. Bak! Bak! Bak! Bak! Bak! The AR was spitting. The driver caught the first shot in the chest and immediately lost control of the Navigator. The SUV. crashed into a parked car.

"Stop! Stop!" Bolo yelled to his little partner behind the wheel. He dashed out of the van towards the SUV. Bobby wasn't hit, but was stuck inside the SUV. His leg was pinned under the dashboard along with his gun. His partner in the back had caught a single shot to the neck and lay dead across the seats from his waist over.

Bolo ran up on the SUV. He didn't even bother to look. Bolo shot a barrage of bullets into the Navigator. Bobby got hit in the leg, and grazed twice, one across the chest and the other in his arm. Bobby slumped over and played dead. Bolo finished with his work, and then sprinted back to the caravan, the little soldiers dashed off from the scene.

Chapter 7

"I took care of that."

"Aight." Nia said and then disconnected the call. She placed the cell back in her purse.

The let out was crazy. Nia stood next to Jonas waiting for their cars to be returned by the valet. The B.O.G. soldiers surrounded them. Jonas occasionally checked out the scantily clad females leaving. But, he couldn't get Bobby's actions out of his head. Jonas didn't want a war. He despised it, at this point in time killing Bobby would definitely guarantee a war between the B.O.G. and the Bogus Boyz even though they lacked the structure. The war in 91-92 between the Black Disciples and the Gangsta Disciples crept up in Jonas's thoughts even though he was a youngster at the time, the history was well known in Chicago. Both made tactical errors that caused a lot of good men to get killed. Jonas didn't want that, Nia had ruled like that, Jonas wouldn't.

Jonas shook his head at the thought. A black Chevy Caprice raced down the streets. All eyes were on the tinted out vehicle. Out of nowhere the car stopped in front of B.O.G.'s small circle of members.

"Oh shit! It's a hit!" yelled Nia as she dropped to the ground. The whole crowd followed when they saw the long

AK 47's muzzle hanging out of the window. The masked man didn't hesitate, the automatic rifle lit the night up. The shooting was brief and then they sped off into the night. Nia jumped up with a nine millimeter in her hand and dashed into the middle of the street dumping hot lead on the car. The back window of the Chevy shattered. Nia kept gunning, the Chevy swerved and crashed into a telephone pole.

Just as Nia was done shooting, the Rolls were pulling up. Trina ran over to the car and got behind the wheel. One of the B.O.G.'s soldiers grabbed Nia and threw her into the vehicle. Jonas leaped up and jumped into the backseat.

Chapter 8

2 days later

J oey ran up the steps. He raced passed the elevator that he would've normally taken to the spot. The hallway was quiet, but weed smoke filled the air. Riverview Condominiums was an upscale place that didn't tolerate any rude, violent or illegal behavior in their living space but, Omar was an exception. He owned a Condo in the place. From his heroin trade and bumping heads with major business professionals in the city, he knew the owner of Riverview well.

He raced down the hallway towards the door. The smell of weed intensified in the air. "BAM!, BAM!, BAM!." Joey banged hard against the door trying to get the attention of the occupants.

Omar swung the door open while holding a sleek, black forty caliber Smith and Wesson. The smell of exotic Kush pushed forward and Joey caught the full contact of the aroma.

" Man, what the fuck is wrong with you?!"

Joey was stuck. Not from fear, but because of his stuttering problem. He only did it when he got really excited.

"O,O,O,O!" Joey said and then stopped himself so he could calm down.

"What you want mutha fucka!" Omar barked at his little brother. He grabbed Joey by the collar and yanked him into the room.

Joey was a tall lanky individual standing at six-six and weighing two hundred and forty-five pounds, he was supposed to be the next Derrick Rose out of Chicago. He had a nice handle and a wicked jump shot that drove the college scouts crazy. Joey had been sought after from some of the top schools in America. Duke, Georgetown, UCCA, North Carolina and Syracuse but he chooses to attend Kentucky. He wanted to be close to home, but still attend a division one school. While preparing for his first year and all of the drama that followed from his star status on the campus, Joey was accused of raping a white girl on the night of homecoming. He was arrested, charged and spend two years in jail. Bobby and Omar helped him get the best lawyers and Joey eventually beat all the charges, but his basketball career was over for good. From a knee injury he caught in jail while playing free rec with the other inmates.

Omar let his grip on Joey loose and walked towards the living room. He had been on the paranoid side ever since he learned about Bobby getting shot.

"What's up Joey?" asked Omar.

"I found out who shot Bobby!" Joey said, calmly.

He had settled down now. Joey's blood was flowing and his mind reacting properly. Omar just stared at him. He didn't really want to know who hit Bobby. The two brothers were completely different. Where Bobby loved the allure of being a gangster, Omar loved the money and being low key about his dealings on the streets. He had gone and visited Bobby this morning and already got the full breakdown of what happened. He just didn't explain it to their little brother, Joey. Omar hated the fact that Joey was robbed of his basketball career, so he tried his best to keep him off of the streets. But, Bobby wouldn't allow it, He brought Joey under his wing and taught him everything about the street life.

By Omar being the oldest out and two at the age of thirty-eight. He felt that they had to abide by his rules. Bobby wouldn't adhere to it though, he always been the rebellious little brother.

He turned away from Joey. Omar placed the gun on his circular glass table. A box of Dutch's and a little over an ounce of lime green marijuana was lumped up in a small pile on the table.

Joanna sat on the edge of the leather seat. The white sofa brought out her chocolate features. She slouched back and raised the Butch to her mouth. Joanna fired the cigar up, and then inhaled deeply.

Joey just stood there with his eyes fixated between Joanna's legs. Her large camel toe stood out in the small boy shorts.

"Boy, what'cha lookin at?" she said, while giggling. Joanna knew little Joey always sized her up every time he came to the Condo.

"Girl go ahead."

Joanna closed her legs and looked at Omar.

"Come on over here, so we can talk."

Omar took the lit cigar from Joanna and walked over to the window. The shades were drawn and a view of Lake Michigan could be seen afar. Joey strolled over to the window next to Omar, although Joey was the tallest amongst the brothers at the tender age of twenty-one. He towered over Omar, who only stood five-ten. What, Omar lacked in the size, he made up for in stature. He was wealthy in his old age.

"So, who did it?" asked Omar.

"Bolo...This little freak I be messing with told me."

"How, she know?" Omar said.

"Because, she was seen when Bolo got into the van around the corner from the club."

"Bobby said, Nia and Jonas was the one's that ran up on them."

"Naw, he got to be mistaken...She seen Bolo with her own eyes...I know she ain't going to lie about something like this."

"Did she tell the police? Or anybody else!"

"Naw, she ain't on it like that...So, what we going to do? We need to let Bobby know about this."

Omar was skeptical about telling Bobby. He just wanted him to chill. Let the beef die down with the B.O.G. and continue selling his heroin on Murders Row. Omar knew Bobby wouldn't have it that way though. He was already having a fit in the hospital about the attempted murder on his life. Bobby was festering with thoughts of revenge and wanted it done quickly.

Omar's thoughts raced. "Listen, everybody got their facts twisted...We know the B.O.G. did it, but we don't know if it really was green lighted by Jonas or Nia...Bolo could've just did it on his own...He is a broad member."

Joey looked at Omar with a confused look.

"Man this is our bloodline right! They just hit Bobby and killed two of our trusted soldiers...We need to clap back immediately."

Omar glanced at Joanna firing up another Dutch.

"Ay, go get ya self together we bout to go take a ride."

He yelled at her. Omar didn't want her to hear this part of the business. Drug dealing was one thing, but murder was a whole different ball game.

Joanna stood up from the sofa. Her pink boy shorts clung between her luscious round booty. She wore a white wife beater that had a small slit down the top, which showed a lot of cleavage. Joanna sashayed towards the hallway. Her ass jiggled with each step she took. She stopped and turned around to ask Omar a question. "What should I wear? Where we going?"

"Girl, just throw some shit on. Don't worry about where we going!"

Omar was mad, he hated when she got high and acted stupid. Joanna only did it when she had weed in her system.

"Whatever punk!" Joanna said, playfully.

She turned to leave, while walking the small shorts rode up between her cheeks. She stopped and reached back to get them out. Joanna turned around and giggled at the two men staring at her ass.

Omar didn't pay her no mind. Joey's eyes lit up. He had always wanted to bang Joanna. He even asked Omar numerous times, he always turned Joey down.

"Ay, we not going to react until we know for sure who made the call...Just chill and let shit play out...I got this."

"Play itself out, man you tripping O. We need to hit them. It was B.O.G. who made the call, period point blank."

"Look, Joey them B.O.G. niggas play for keeps. I had been dealing with Nia and Jonas since you were a snotty nose ball player."

"I'm going to gather some of the homies up and we going to go see them B.O.G. niggas."

"Joey! Leave that alone. Right now you're emotional and it's a common feeling to want to lash out like that, but you got to be smart and we need to think this thing all the way through." said Omar.

He knew that he really couldn't contain Joey. Bobby had his head twisted with all of this delusional gangster stuff and dying for a stupid cause, for a gang that in the end didn't account to nothing, but either a life sentence or an early death.

Omar thought about switching gears on Joey, but declined. Joey was too far gone at this point. 'I'm going to have to get Bobby to calm him down before it's too late.' He thought to himself.

"I understand." Joey said.

He didn't really mean it though. Joey just wanted Omar to shut up. "Bobby always told me that the more money you had, the softer you got." Joey mumbled real low.

Omar didn't catch the smart remark.

Chapter 9

The gang unit within the Chicago Police Department had been assigned to the shooting, and the two deaths of the Bogus Boys. Detective Patrick Shaw a.k.a. The Night Stalker had run the unit for the past eight years. The Night Stalker had taken down a lot of major gangs with them over the years. Black Disciples, New Breeds, Four Corner Hustlers, Mafia Insane and a host of others that dealt, during the glory years. A lot of the times, he took down key members, but the cycled still continued. You always had somebody else willing to take over leadership and the groups would always bounce back. Some stronger than others, but this was the reason Patrick was always hard work. Chicago's gang culture was firmly rooted in place and not leaving anytime soon no matter how many Night Stalkers you had on the Chicago P.D.

Detective Shaw was an imposing man. He stood six-four and weighed two hundred and thirty five pounds. The Night Stalker worked his size to his advantage. Although, he was a white man, Detective Shaw wasn't intimidated by the dangerous crack- infested neighborhoods of Chicago.

The Night Stalker had been frustrated, as of late he had been working on the double homicide for three weeks and still hadn't come up with any witness leads or any other vital information to help him pin point the murderer or murderers. But, he did have some information about a party that took place that night. So, that's where his investigation was stuck at. There was a party hosted by the Blackout gang, and Bobby Mackey had an altercation with Jonas, but that was it. An argument wouldn't necessarily lead to murder, he thought, but the night stalker knew their leader, Nia well.

The Night Stalker was slouched over at his desk with a bunch of crime scene photographs. He stopped looking at the photos and glanced up at his partner.

"This is the Black Out's work."

"Why would you say that? We don't have any evidence pointing to them." Nakira said, a bit defensive.

Nakira Whitehurst sat at her desk across fromThe Night Stalker. She was new to the infamous gang unit. The Chief of Police had personally placed her inside the unit. He wanted The Night Stalker to show her around and break her into the unit. So, for the past year, Nakira had been partnered up with Detective Shaw.

The Chief placed her in the unit for a reason. Detective Whitehurst was from Englewood. She grew up in the neighborhood and had come from a large family of drug dealers and street hustlers. The Chief figured that Nakira could probably gain a fast hold in the area unlike some of his other gang unit officers. She knew people and they respected her a lot around the neighborhood. Let alone, she was black. Most of the other members were either white or Spanish.

Detective Shaw looked at Whitehurst with a surprised, but determined look. "Those files your reading over there."

He pointed his thick fingers at the crime scene photos taking of the two dead occupants in a black Chevy Caprice.

"What gangs do they belong too?"

Nakira already knew where Detective Shaw was going with the evidence.

"Bogus Boys."

"Bobby Mackey is their so-called leader. He gets shot and almost killed while his two little flunkies in the car with him get killed right around the corner from these other murders."

"That still doesn't mean that the Black Out Gang had anything to do with it."

"Detective Whitehurst you're a smart lady...Now, let's play this out...Bobby leaves the club angry over something. He and two other men get into a SUV. They get shot at over twenty times from an AR-15 and they also have automatic rifles in the vehicle with them...Five minutes later, Bogus Boys members try to kill Nia outside of the club, but somehow a person kills them instead."

Nakira just sat there acting confused, but yet concerned with solving the case; she had already put the two incidents together. When she interviewed some stragglers at the crime scene, everybody declined to speak or acted like they didn't know anything.

"I understand. We should go talk to Bobby then."

"We already know what his answer is going to be, so I'm not going to even waste our time."

The Night Stalker reached for the photos and a few statements Nakira had. He stared at them hard, The Night Stalker was convinced now. The Black Out Gang had something to do with this. He could not shake the feeling, but feeling it was one thing, solving it was another.

Chapter 10

W hite, sheer linen curtains were spread wide open, so the full view of Chicago's country side could be seen through Jonas's bedroom window. A spectacular view consisting of an assortment of maple, oak, and pine trees and a mix of beautiful flowers were scattered as far as you could see, in any direction.

Jonas lay back in the bed. With just a thin white sheet covering his lower body, he sat there contemplating his next move. Jonas had been laying low since Bobby got hit and four of his Bogus Boys were killed. He was furious that Nia reacted in such a stupid way.

He scolded Nia about her vicious actions. It had only been three and a half weeks since he had been home and the B.O.G. was responsible for four senseless murders. Jonas had planned to deal with Bobby in a different way. He had a repone with Bobby's brother, Omar and thought that they could settle the little disagreement through the right channels, but Nia had different plans.

Jonas turned slightly to puff his pillow. It had been all smashed in and messed up from the long love making session he had with Yvonne. After fluffing the pillows and placing them up against the tall wooden frame on the back of the bed, he laid back down.

The room smelled slightly of sex and Chanel number 5. Yvonne had hurried out of the bed to go shower and get dressed. She had been racing back and forth to the bathroom putting on her clothes and spraying a fine mist of perfume on herself. Yvonne was in a rush to make it to work. She had missed the last week laying around the condo with Jonas. Jonas just smiled as she ran back and fourth.

"Ay, Yvonne run some bath water for me before you leave."

She stormed out of the bathroom with a half-smile. The petite lady stood five-three, but her heels gave her an additional three inches. Yvonne was dressed simply in a red Herve Leger skin tight skirt. Her brown skin complexion and shoulder length black hair made Yvonne look like a princess. Yvonne rested both hands loosely on her hips.

"Jonas." she whined. "Why are you trying to make me late?"

Jonas couldn't help but to smile at the little lady. Yvonne was his little rider; she had done the last three years of Jonas's bid with him. They had met prior to incarceration and went out a couple of times together, and then he got locked up for the murder. Jonas had let her go. He had fifty years and couldn't deal with the long distance relationship. Yvonne tried to ignore his requests, but then she went on about her life. At the time she was twenty-five and still trying to find herself in life. Yvonne did just that. Found herself, she went on and enrolled into the Fashion Institute of Atlanta, where she studied hard to design clothes. Yvonne had dreams of starting her own clothing line. She had the dream since she was a little girl. Yvonne graduated from the school and interned a couple of years with Roca Wear,

Apple Bottoms and Sean Johns clothing lines before moving back to Chicago.

She went back to the Go and got a job as the design director for Street Dreamz clothing company. When she was fully set into her career and had a steady job, Yvonne reached back out to Jonas. At the time, Jonas was just starting the process of gathering all the information for his past-conviction motion, based on newly discovered evidence.

"Okay, I'll do it...Don't worry about it sweetheart." Jonas replied.

Yvonne rushed back into the bathroom to finish applying her makeup. The tight skirt had risen a little from her curvy hips switching to the side. Jonas placed his hands behind his head and stretched his huge body over the King-size bed. He gazed straight up at the ceiling. Jonas had developed a liking for Yvonne, but he knew it wouldn't work. She constantly badgered him about leaving the gang life, apparently Yvonne thought she had it all planned out. She wanted to start a clothing line within a few years, marry Jonas and live happily ever after. That wasn't Jonas's plan. He had on numerous occasions tried to break it down to her. First, that he wasn't leaving B.O.G. alone and second that he wasn't ready for marriage. Jonas was only thirty-five and did ten long years. Marriage was the last thing on his mind. He had decided today would be the day to break off their little relationship, but every time he tried to talk about it, Yvonne stopped him as if she knew what he was up too.

The phone ringing brought Jonas out of his thoughts. He reached over to the wooden table and snatched up the phone. Jonas glanced at the block number.

"What's up?"

"Ay, Jonas this is Omar. What's good with you?" He tried to sound polite.

"I'm good."

"Yeah, I got ya number from a mutual friend."

Omar stopped. He was trying to find the right words to say. "I wanted to know if we could get together and put this problem behind us."

"I was thinking the same thing. How's ya brother taking this though! Are you speaking for him and the Bogus Boys?"

Omar was stuck. He couldn't speak for Bobby or his gang. Omar just supplied them with drugs, he didn't get into all of the gangs politics. But something had to be done in order to stop a full scale war that Bobby was going to bring.

"Now, Jonas you know I'm not a gang member, I left that shit alone when we were still kids, so I'm not speaking on behalf of them. I could care less about some gang shit. I'm calling on the strength of my brother. I plan on speaking to him when he gets released this week. I'm going to try and persuade him to leave all this shit alone."

"I hope so Omar...I hope so."

"I need a guarantee from you though." Omar said.

"What?"

"Call the wolves off for a little, so I can talk some sense into him we both know how hot-headed he can get. But, I can convince him. By the way, y'all got money to make and we got money to make. Aint no sense to drawing any

unwanted attention to either of us behind this stupid shit."
Omar said.

Jonas nodded his head in agreement with Omar's
statement. He felt the same way.

"So, when do you want to meet?"

"A week and a half."

"Aight." replied Jonas.

He finished the call with a couple of seconds of small
talk and then disconnected the line. Jonas tossed the phone
down beside him. He, then stared up at the ceiling again.

Yvonne stormed out of the bathroom, looking sexier
than ever. She strutted over to Jonas and kissed him
passionately on the lips. "I hope that wasn't one of your
gang flunkies." She said, and then strolled out of the room.
Jonas shook his head in disgust at her comment.

Chapter 11

Nia's Benz rolled up to the red light on 66th and Ashland Street. She sat on the passenger's side with her phone glued to her ear. The cold, black steel of a Taurus nine millimeter laid across her skimpy, denim shorts by Juicy Couture. She played with the gun, as she talked on the phone.

Trina was behind the wheel. She checked the mirror every twenty seconds due to her growing paranoia and her slight vanity. . She knew first hand the streets played no games and if you got caught slipping that was your ass period. The awareness came from being around her brother Low-low a lot. He was a hired gun in Chicago. Low-low, as they called him based in part on him being low key, and then claiming to have the ability to determine anyone's fate. Throughout Chicago, it was estimated that he killed thirty people himself without being paid by anyone to do so. He had trained Trina in the art. Low-low had showed her firsthand how to kill by the knife and gun, and then get away with it. She grasped it easily and became one of the best at the young age of twenty-one. That was the greatest gift her brother ever gave her. She would brag to Nia about it. Nia knew about Low-low's work real well she had paid for his assistance on one occasion when it was impossible for her to get a nigga, on this particular assignment. He brought Trina to the meeting he was having with Nia, and, the two girls clicked ever since. They got so tight that people started to think that they were lovers or something. But, it wasn't like that. They both just loved the hustle, the gun totting, busting and all the other fame that being a gangster brought into your life.

"I love you baby. Sorry I missed our weekly visit. It been kinda crazy around here lately." said Nia. She smiled to herself, as she talked in a baby like voice to her childhood sweetheart, Mark.

Trina elbowed Nia real hard to get her attention. She didn't want to say it out loud while she was still on the phone. Nia gave her a thuggish look. She sensed the trouble in Trina's eyes gazing through her rearview mirror. Trina never bothered to stare at Nia. She said her last good byes to Mark and hung the phone up.

Nia rub her arm and asked, "bitch why you hit me so hard."

"Black Yukon! It keep moving in and out of traffic like its trying to get close to us."

Nia leaned up to look out of the passenger side mirror. The Yukon was moving its way forward. She gripped her gun tightly. Nia watched the Yukon intently now. She was trying to see who the driver was and if they had any passengers in the truck. The light turned green Trina hesitated for a second and reached underneath her seat. She pulled out a black and gray Tec-9. Trina lifted the gun up and placed it on her lap. She hit the gas lightly. The two was ready for blood, and there was no backing down. This is what they loved, gun play.

"The nigga got a ski-mask, Tray!"

"I see em, I see em!"

She slows the Benz up a little.

"I'm going to pull over at this next parking spot, get ready to move."

"Bitch come on!" Nia said, a bit anxious to bust her gun.

Trina jerked over to the curb quickly. Nia tried to leap out of the Benz, but it was too late. The Black Yukon sped up and pulled on the side of her. The Yukon window was already down, and the masked gunman already had a silver Desert Eagle out of the window. "BOOM! BOOM! BOOM!" The loud shots echoed off the buildings. The first blast went straight through the driver window, and logged in the dash board. Nia dove out of the passenger seat and out of the way of the gunfire. She was wearing Sandals, a printed white t-shirt and skimpy denim shorts, she scraped her knees and elbows. Nia didn't care though, she was determined to fight.

The second and third blasts from the fifty caliber went into the back doors of the pretty white Benz. Trina was stuck for a second, once she heard the shooter hesitate on firing she upped her Kel-Tec. she let the fifty shot semi-automatic rip. Nia slide behind the Benz and started firing. She was hitting everything on the Yukon except the passenger side door, and window. She understood what she was doing. Nia and Trina had been in plenty of shoot-outs together over their fifteen year relationship as friends. Nia was making sure nobody in the back jumped out the SUV or the passenger continue shooting at Trina.

Bak! Bak! Bak! Bak! Bak! Trina continued firing, while holding both hands on the gun. She hit the whole passenger door up. The Yukon sped off. Nia stepped into the street, and continued shooting until her gun locked back. She looked at the 9mm and ran to the passenger side door. Glass and shells covered the cream leather seats. Nia, quickly plopped down on the seat.

"GO! GO!" Nia yelled at Trina who was busy checking herself for any wounds.

Finally, happy that she was unscathed, Trina punched on the gas. The two women were high off of adrenaline. They both remained quiet trying to come back to their senses and out of that zone. The death zone. The zone that made you think quickly about how you were going to either die or fight harder in order for you to be victorious.

"Who you think that was?"

"Nia, I don't know, but I'm sure about one thing. Nobody has tried us like that in a long time."

"Right!"

"So it had to be them Bogus Boyz."

"I think so too." Said Nia, she gazed out of the window.

Nias mind was made up. They had to go whether Jonas wanted war or not. She was going to kill them, every last one. Jonas wanted to make money in peace, but killing comes with the price of having power and control. Nia understood the later clearly. She just had to convince her big brother that wars create peace and the war was definitely on.

Chapter 12

The Englewood section of Chicago was considered one of the most dangerous places in America. It was where the bulk of Chicago's murders took place and it was also the birthplace of two of the biggest gangs. That city of Chicago has ever seen, and they were the Black Out Gang, and the Gangsta Disciples. Both of their leaders hailed from this place. Larry from Halsted St. and Jonas came up on 66th and Justine Street.

On the long city block of 66th and Justine Street was where Jonas's big brother, Big Ant, once walked the pavements banging, hustling and doing anything else to get a dollar. The place was surrounded by abandoned buildings, homes and huge vacant lots. That made it a magnet for drug activity. The place had been dubbed 'Hustlers Row' from the constant flow of fiends frequenting the place trying to get their next fix and niggas hugging the block hustling.

Big Ant had grinded on the street for years and made a lot of money before he took three headshots from a dope fiend at five-thirty in the morning trying to get a fix. The strip was legendary from the turf fights, as well as from the police trying to gain control over the area. Cocaine Curtis, who was considered one of the hardest gangstas to come out of Englewood was gunned down by Chicago P.D. for no reason, other than the fact that he was making too much money and refused to pay off the crooked cops that patrolled the neighborhood. They had planned to set him up one day and raided Hustler's Row. Cocaine Curtis, knew the raid was a sham, so when the police hit the street and some young hustlers started running to get away, the cops just start shooting at the fleeing youngsters. They then focused their weapons on Curtis, but he was already on the point. Cocaine Curtis fired on the cops. He killed two in the process but he was also lost his life.

The names of hustlers was endless that contributed to the street's history. Danny Price was another one. The younger, charismatic nigga got rich and that made him a lot of enemies. He didn't care, though, he was a goon. Gangsta-Gun-Slinger or any other definition you would give a person who was down for whatever. Danny sold a lot of heroin and also dabbled in the extortion business. He had put the full court press on the leader of the 'Breeds'. He was getting paid a kilogram of cocaine a month from him, the equivalent at the time, which was twenty-five stacks. The leader of the Breeds was sick of it, so he hired some out of town killers to hollaat Danny. The group of two men followed Danny home to one of his houses in the suburbs and waited outside for him. Danny came out of his home late at night taking the trash out and the two hit-men jumped out, and unloaded on him. Danny did manage to get a shot off and hit one of the men in the stomach before taking two shots in the head.

Jonas was well-aware of the stories and incidents that took place on the 66th and Justine. They were his stomping grounds. He sold his first batch of drugs on the corner, turned his first trick at the age of twelve on the street and even made the place one off his biggest money making spots. Jonas had picked up, where all the others from the past had left behind. When Marc Anthony set him up with the shipments, Hustler's Row was the first spot that he got Nia to lock down. She had helped though, from other B.O.G. members.

Black smoke had been giving control over the North side, but Jonas was also giving him the authority to run Hustler's Row. The spot had been Nia's, but upon release from prison Jonas decided to take it from her. She had gotten to wild, he had thought. Jonas didn't want his major spot getting any unwanted attention from the authorities. He had explained to her the reasons for taking the street back. It wasn't anything personal and she understood. Nia was glad actually. The place had been a lot of stress for her to keep up with. Nia just wanted to take a back seat on continuing monitoring the strip.

The sky was light blue and the sun was shining brightly. It was the beginning of summer, so Hustler's Row was heavy with activity. Black Smoke stood against the light pole talking to the high yellow female. She was dressed scantily with orange cotton shorts that stopped right at her cheeks and cut sharply into her vagina. Her black shirt came just to her navel, and had the "Baddest Bitch" in orange written across it in cursive, with a pair of black flip-flops to match her outfit.

The hustlers were out and cars lined up to get served. Black Smoke was just out there chilling with the youngsters. He didn't have anything lined up for the afternoon. Zombie looking fiends walked up and down the sidewalk, while B.O.G. members roamed them to. Some were on security; others went hand-to-hand serving the zombies.

"Rocks and Blows!" A youngster yelled.

He stopped and another line formed in front of him on the sidewalk.

"Have your money in your hands and keep your hands out of your pockets!" yelled another B.O.G. member, who was strictly on security.

Black Smoke heard the reminder and glanced at the fiends lining up. Smoke knew how easy it was to get hit on Hustler's row. He knew the history and understood the environment all to well.

"Watch those cars and keep the traffic moving!" yelled the same B.O.G. member.

The cars and trucks had started to jam the street. This was a no-no. The rule was to keep everything and everybody moving. No pulling up and stopping to talk. It wasn't any time for that. Money was to be made, all the talking and playing could take place after the last pack was sold for the day, other than that business had to be finished.

B.O.G. had the place locked down. Black Smoke had placed shooters on the roof tops and some of the young soldiers patrolled the strip armed with guns. He even went so far as to have one of the B.O.G. youngster's stand in the middle of traffic scoping out suspicious cars that needed to be pulled over. The youngster carried a gun and a grenade on him just in case he was in trouble and needed a quick getaway.

A red Ducati sped up behind a green van. The shooter, who stood on the two story roof yelled. "Watch that bike! Watch that bike."

The motorcycle was occupied by two people. The youngster, who scouted the vehicles didn't hear the man on the roof. The bike moved at a snail's pace moving along the line to get served.

KD, a B.O.G. member whose job was to serve the cars and trucks was busy at the top of the block, serving a person in the car. Smoke stood twenty feet away from him still chatting with the young girl. The bike made its way towards KD. The high yellow woman had shifted her body slightly to the side of Smoke. He laughed and joked with her.

The passenger on the bike fiddled a little bit with the driver shirt in the back. He grabbed the Cold forty-five, as the bike was slowly moving up in the line, he slung the gun around and immediately shot. "Boom, Boom, Boom, Boom, Boom!" The semi-automatic dazed everybody. Smoke got hit twice in the chest. Rivulets of blood spilled onto his white t-shirt turning it red quickly, as he leaned against the telephone pole for support, then he dropped head first onto the ground. The red bone yelled at the side. She dove behind a parked car trying her best to get away from the assassins.

Sid, on the roof, was heard. "Damn! Damn!" He quickly put the shooter in his sights. After, the third shot from the passenger on the bike, Sid fired two rounds out of the 30/30 rifle. The first shot grazed the shooters left shoulder, and the second went straight through his helmet and penetrated the side of a parked car, which left a nice size hole.

The zombies ran from all of the confusion while, everybody else took cover and brandished their guns. B.O.G. was on full alert now. When the driver felt his partner's head land on his back and saw him drop his gun, he pulled the throttle back fast. The Ducati lifted up and took off. Several members from the **B.O.G** ran out in the street shooting at the motorcycle, but he was long gone.

Chapter 13

A father's love for his daughter is special. Jonas always thought. So therefore he treated everything that dealt with Tia as a special moment. Tia had been born a day before Jonas's arrest. He was twenty five years old, at the time and thuggin hard. Jonas held her on the first day of her birth and made a vow to her, a vow that only they knew. It was to cherish, pamper, provide and to protect her from all of life's crazy twists and turns. He tried to uphold his end, but incarceration hindered a lot of his progress. Jonas took care of Tia, her whole life. By him hustling in the joint, Nia holding B.O.G. down and having access to plenty of narcotics; Jonas managed to provide everything she ever asked for. The little girl loved the gifts, but she longed for her daddy to come home.

On one particular day, Jonas called her. They talked for almost an hour, the two laughed and talked about all the little things that a five year old would at the time. After hanging up the phone, Tia went and packed her clothes with a couple of toys. Lisa walked passed her room and saw the little girl packing and asked why. She just told her that it was a surprise. Lisa didn't think nothing of it because Nia would often come get her for weekends and the two would fly out to Las Vegas, where Nia's boyfriend lived. Tia waited on the couch for hours with her suitcase packed. Lisa was curious why Nia was taking so long, so she called her. Nia told Lisa that she wasn't taking Tia anywhere. Lisa then went and asked Tia again where she was going. Tia told her that her daddy was coming to get her. Lisa was furious. Jonas had fifty years. There was no way he was going to be able to take her anywhere. She explained everything to Tia.

She cried for days. Tia misunderstood the conversation she had with Jonas. He never told her such a thing. When Jonas called a week later Lisa refused to let him speak to her. Jonas was crushed, not because of the actions that Lisa done, but because Tia had really believed he was coming to get her. He explained to Tia on many of occasions, the possibility of him not being able to see her again. She didn't understand though.

Jonas pulled into the driveway of Lisa's house. Tia had been waiting patiently for him to arrive. Today was their day. After, the argument he had with Lisa, Jonas had called her later that day and talked to Tia. He made a promise that Saturday's were her day. She could do anything she wanted to do with daddy. Jonas looked at it as this was the least he could do. He was trying to make up for the ten years he lost with her.

Tia saw the black looking Batman mobile pull up. She ran off the small step to greet her father. Jonas was barely out of the driver's door when the pretty little girl jumped into his arm. He caught Tia and they held one another for what felt and eternity, Then Jonas planted a kiss on her forehead.

"How is my princess today? You look so beautiful."

Tia smiled at the remark "Thank you daddy and I'm happy to see you."

Jonas sees Lisa stroll out on to the front steps. He gently placed Tia on her feet. The little girl beamed with joy. Her dreams had come true. Daddy was finally home and spending time with her. Tia moved around the car. Her hair was black and long but pulled back into a pony tail. She had on a pair of white AirForce 1's, a pair of colorful plaid polo shorts with a matching t-shirt.

Lisa stood there watching the two. She held both hands on her hips. Lisa really didn't despise Jonas, she was just upset that he didn't want her no more. She understood his reasons even though she didn't agree with them.

"Take care of my baby," said Lisa.

She leaned up against the bricks on the frame of the house and poked her hip out intentionally. Lisa had on a tight-fitting mini-skirt, a white sleeveless t-shirt by Gucci and red stiletto's. She looked stunning, just to be going to work. Jonas thought, as he looked over at her. She caught his stare and gave him a flirtatious smile, biting her bottom lip. Jonas knew better though.

"I got her. I'm going to talk to you later."

"Okay. Love you sweetheart, bye." said Lisa. She waved at Tia.

"Bye Mommy." Tia waved back.

Tia hopped into the passenger seat of the Maserati. Once fully inside, Jonas closed the door behind her. He then walked around the car heading toward the driver's side.

"Can you call me later on?" Lisa asked.

"For what?" Jonas asked a bit angry.

"Jonas, stop being mean to me all the time. Damn! You know I still love you."

Jonas continued moving. He didn't even bother to glance at Lisa. He knew his weaknesses for her. Jonas wasn't trying to fall victim again.

"I'll think about it. I'm still messed up about that stunt you pulled a few month's back." He said, stopping at the door.

"I'm sorry. I was jealous and mad at you...You know how I get at times." She said, with a childish tone.

"Yeah, I know. I'll holla at you later."

Jonas got into the car. Lisa was stuck on the wall. She was frustrated, mad and upset that she had done such a stupid thing, which put her in the current predicament. The one-night stand she had with Paris was nothing. It all was really a blur to her but it did happen.

The day at the shop had been hectic. It was a big show in the town. Kanye and his Music Group were performing at the Navy Pier. The who's who of Chicago had flooded Lisa's salon with appointments. Lisa and her five girl crew went to work. They finished all the heads by ten o'clock, and then they all hurried home to get dressed for the show. Lisa and her crew made it to the show. They partied and even got backstage to kick it with Kayne and his crew, with the help of Nia.

After the show, Nia threw an after party at the restaurant "Fifty Yard Line". Liquor was flowing, marijuana clouded the air and the crew was having a good time. Half of Chicago had come out to party and show support for one of their own. So, the scene was relaxed and the gangs at ease for the night.

Lisa had gotten so drunk and partied hard. Nia noticed her staggering around the place and had Paris, a Broad member at the time, watch over Lisa and take her home. She couldn't leave Lisa to herself, and Jonas would've been pissed if Nia didn't look after her.

Paris grabbed Lisa up and dragged her out of the party, Paris was not really a looker but he still had a lot of say in the B.O.G. He got Lisa in the car and left the club.

Paris was drunk himself. Lisa sat in the seat and flirted, talking dirty and even began rubbing all over Paris's body. He tried to stop her plenty of times but Lisa wore him down. Lisa fondled him while driving all the way to her house in Hype Park. Finally at her house, Paris pulled into the driveway. He leaned back in the seat enjoying the hand treatment. She started to go down on him but he grabbed her hair. Lisa looked confused. She snatched his keys out of the ignition and forced Paris to come inside her house and Paris followed.

Tia had been gone for the weekend. She was staying with Lisa's parents, so the house was completely empty. Paris stepped into the house behind Lisa. He closed the door and the two immediately stripped down. They got completely naked and had sex right there in the living room.

The party had ended and Nia was looking for Paris. She had sent him to take Lisa home and he never return. She paid it no mind. Nia went home for the night. The next morning Nia got up early, she had an appointment with Lisa to get her hair done. Nia figured she'd swing by Lisa's house for breakfast, and then they would go to the salon right after they ate. Nia pulled up to the house. Paris's car was still parked in the driveway. She got out of her car and headed to the house. Nia started to knock on the door but she felt a little vibe that told her to go check the window first. Nia stepped over to the living room window squinting her eyes to peek through the tiny cracks of the curtains. Her heart dropped when she saw Lisa and Paris sleeping together naked on the sofa. At first, she wanted to kick the door down and hit both of them but then she thought about Tia. Nia went and banged on the door. Lisa woke up first. She looked over at Paris and felt disquieted. Lisa didn't even bother to wake him up. She hurried up and put her clothes back on. Fully dressed, she went and opened the door without even looking to see who it was. Lisa froze when she saw the rage in Nia's intense green eyes. Nia pushed her aside and stormed into the house. Paris still was sleeping, Nia ran over to him and slapped the life out of him. Paris woke up angry, swearing and ready for blood, until he realized it was Nia in front of him. Nia just shock her head and stomped out of the house. Paris knew he was in some deep shit. He witnessed Nia's work first hand. He knew that only two options remained for him. Either skip town or take the B.O.G. to war. Paris leaned more to the latter. Taking the B.O.G to war was dangerous, and he knew it. Paris knew what they were capable of doing. At one point, he was one of the ones giving orders to go kill some of their enemies. Sleeping with any member's girl was not good.

Nia sped off and called Trina up. She broke everything down for Trina. They decided, then and there that Paris had to go immediately. The girls meet up on a side-street. Trina had bought an AR-15 with her, and was driving a stolen Dodge Ram truck. They headed straight to Paris's apartment in Englewood Terrace. Trina parked down the street from his complex. Paris sped up and parked between the two cars inside the complex. Nia spotted him first, Trina pulled up on Paris, slowly from his backside. He didn't even bother to look at the vehicle because of him being in such a rush to get into his apartment. Nia leaped out of the truck, she wore a black silk scarf around her face, to conceal her identity. Nia shouted out Paris's name. He froze. She lifted the automatic weapon and peppered Paris with hot lead, tearing his flesh apart. He fell to the pavement and Nia ran over top of him. She unloaded twenty shots between his head and torso. The girls escaped without even being noticed.

Paris's murder was so gruesome that he had to have a closed casket funeral. Paris's face had melted to the ground from the ten shots. Lisa was terrified. She begged and pleaded with Jonas for forgiveness. And, also to call Nia off of her, Lisa knew it was just a matter of time before she was killed for her own betrayal. Jonas did the right thing and called it off, but he would never forget the sin that she had committed.

Chapter 14

Jonas drove into the parking garage of Holy Cross Hospital. The hospital had an eight tier garage that could hold plenty of visitors.

He found a parking spot on the second tier and parked. Jonas and Tia walked hand-and-hand towards the hospital's entrance.

Holy Cross flowed with activity on a sunny Saturday morning. Nurses, Doctors and family members strolled around holding quiet conversations to themselves or with their companions. Usually, Jonas would've come by himself to visit his mother. It had been his routine since coming home from prison. Jonas figured that this was there special time together. But, Tia had been asking about Grandmom D for a while. So, he decided to bring her on their special day.

Doris lay quietly in the bed with an IV attached to her arm. Her eyes were slightly closed. She wasn't asleep, just resting in a medicated type of state. Doris had learned this helped ease the pain at times. These were also the times when she reminisced on her life.

At the age of eighteen, Doris left Ashville, North Carolina for the big city of Chicago. Doris had big dreams of going to the city and becoming a Blue's singer. With that goal Doris went and found work at the famous Cotton Club.

The Cotton Club at the time was where all the hustlers, pimps and gangsters frequented. It was the place to be, if you were important. She quickly caught the eye of a major hustler named William Diary. He was a fast talker from Chicago. After a few months of courting her, the two became an item. Within a few years the couple had two boys, Mike "Big Ant" and Jonas. Mike was the first and Jonas Followed. A couple years later, they had Nia. The family was happy for some years to come, but William had a way with women.

William got involved with a woman named Carmen. She was a fellow resident of the city and frequented the Cotton Club, also. William fast talked her, so he thought, and lured Carmen to the local Motel for the night for some serious love making. The two had been going at it for a half-hour. William got up to use the bathroom and when he returned, two men were in the room with guns drawn on him. They tied him up, and made William call for some money. He was being held for a ransom. Everybody knew that he was making a lot of money selling heroin on the streets. William called Doris to bring two hundred thousand, to the pre-determined location. She was a good wife and did as she was told. The kidnappers got the money, and slit William's throat then dropped him off in an alleyway.

Doris was crushed, but she maintained her sanity. She had too, she had kids to raise. Doris had always warned William about stepping out on her and it came back to haunt him in the most egregious way. Doris moved on and established her own hustle in the streets of Chicago. The ol'backwood country girl learned how to survive on her own. It was hard, but she held her own. Doris sold weed, heroin and even opened a boot legging business that sold liquor, wine and spirits after-hours. She even ran a gambling house.

Jonas and Tia walked hand-and-hand down the crowded hall. Nurses strolled around with clip boards in their hands, while some patients sat outside their rooms with family and doctors. Jonas never cared much for hospitals and funeral homes. He tried to avoid them both, at all cost.

A large sign hung above the entrance of the corridor that read: Cancer Ward.

Jonas looked down at Tia and asked, "You ready to see Grandmom D?"

She smiled and nodded her head, yes. This was the first time Tia would ever see her in this state. Doris had declined many of her friends and family from seeing her in such a weak state. Doris hated weakness, so she made damn sure wasn't seen this way.

Tia clutched a dozen of roses in her hand. She was sad and happy. She was sad about her grandmom being sick. Yet happy that she was spending time with her daddy.

They entered the room. Every time Jonas walked into the room to see her, his heart sank and his mind filled with dread. Not fear, but dread. He dreaded the fact that he missed ten productive years with her.

Doris's room was bright, the shades had been pulled back and a view of Marqutte Park, along with Holy Cross's parking lot could be seen. She occupied a room to herself, so there was only her bed in the room. An oxygen tank stood beside the bed and a heart monitor machine. The Nurse had her back turned and was fixing Doris's pillow. Doris saw Tia first and a big smile stretched across her face.

"Is that my baby?" Doris said.

"Yeah. Hey grand mom." Tia said.

Angela turned around with a smile on her face. "Oh, are those roses for me?" asked Angela.

"No these are for my grandmom."

Jonas and Tia strolled over to Doris's bedside. He checked the chocolate nurse out, but blocked the image out of his mind.

Angela walked over to the little girl and squatted down to her level. "You're so pretty. What's your name?"

"Thank you, my name is Tia."

"My name is Amanda." She lied. Angela had been placed here in undercover capacity, as a nurse. Jonas had been visiting his mother twice a week since being released. The DEA had figured that would be the best way to gain access.

Jonas and Doris watched the interaction of the two and just smiled. Tia was sweet like that. Her adorable smile and nice manners attracted many, but she also had the stubborn side that obviously came from the Jonas family.

Angela stood back up and stared at Jonas.

"Ms. Jonas, I'm going to leave now, do you need anything else before I go?"

"No, go ahead child. I'm fine."

"Okay. Nice to meet y'all...Bye Tia." Angela said, while leaving the room.

Angela's cover was perfect, she really was qualified to be a nurse. Angela had went to Seattle University and majored in Nursing. She graduated and was on the way to do her residence when the September 11th bombing happened. Angela decided then and there that she wanted to help. She went and joined the Drug Enforcement Academy. The Agency knew her credentials well and placed her in the right position.

"Mommy, she's been begging to come see you." Jonas said.

Jonas pulled two cushioned seats up to the side of Doris's bed. She looked weak,

Doris had lost close to twenty pounds since being admitted three months ago. Tia leaned over and kissed Doris on the cheek.

"You're so beautiful."

Doris eyes lit up with joy. Nobody had told her that she looked beautiful in months. The cancer had been spreading rapidly through her body and the Chemo wasn't really helping her that much. Her once yellow complexion was now darkening up, and her hair was constantly falling out.

She reached out and grabbed Tia's hand." You're so sweet baby."

"What the doctors say?" Jonas asked.

"Child, I don't know." mumbled Doris

"This is for you." Tia placed the roses next to Doris in her bed.

A soft knock at the door caught everybody's attention. Angela peaked through before fully entering the room.

"Ms. Jonas, I'm leaving for the day so I'll see you tomorrow. And I will bring you some more of that ice cream you like."

"Thank you, honey."

"My number is on the desk, if you need to talk or anything else." Angela said and then kissed Doris on the forehead.

"Take care and don't be so hard on the next shift."

Doris waved her hand to shrug off, Angela's last comment, it was true, Doris had been tuff on everybody. The pain along with the chemo and other prescribed drugs she was taking for the pain had Doris going off on them at times.

Angela glanced at Jonas indiscreetly and quickly turned her head. She didn't want to seem obvious, but she was trying to get his attention.

"Excuse me, can I have a minute of your time?" Jonas said.

She glanced at her watch, "I need to pick my daughter up, so you're going to have to make it quick."

Jonas guided her into the hallway.

"Thanks for looking after my Mom. I know she can be kinda of hard on people at times."

"You said your mane was?"

"Excuse me, I'm Paul Jonas." said Jonas.

He held out his hand gesturing for a handshake Angela accepted it and they both smiled at the awkward introduction.

"Amanda Peterson." Angela replied. "Anyway, I'm just doing my job, so there's no need to thank me."

Angela's pretty smile and innocent look captivated Jonas. She looked like a nice down-to-earth woman, who had a lot going for her.

"I hope this doesn't come off as being immature or inappropriate, but could I take you out to dinner?" Jonas said.

She blushed at the request. Her youthful smile and little girl shyness intrigued Jonas.

"I don't know about dinner, but I'll tell you what. My number is on the desk, give me a call and we could take it from there."

"Fair enough." Jonas said, with a big smile.

He liked her type already. She was conscious and didn't rush to make a decision.

"Take care Paul." Angela said and then strolled away.

He stared at Angela strutting down the hall. Jonas shook his head at how beautiful the woman was, and then walked back into the room.

"Where's your sister?" Doris asked.

"She good, I spoke with her this morning. She should be out here later to see you."

"I'm scheduled for Chemo tomorrow...It's so painful and they say the cancer is eating my pancreas away."

A lone tear rolled down Doris's face. This was the first time she broke; it was an unusual site for Jonas. All of his life nothing ever made his mother cry, except for when William was murdered.

Jonas grabbed her hand. "Mom, you going to pull through this. Remember when you use to tell me. You're a Jonas, there's nothing you can't conquer."

Doris gave him a half hearted smile.

"You'll be fine granny. I talk to God about you every night."

A nurse entered the room and stepped over to the front of the bed.

"Good afternoon Ms. Jonas. The Doctor would like another scan this evening."

"Mommy, we'll be back tomorrow." He kisses her on the cheek and takes her hand. "Be strong." Jonas whispered in her ear.

"You be safe out there, and watch after my baby now." Doris said.

No matter how dangerous Jonas was, or how old he got Doris still looked at him as her baby. Jonas loved his mom, so he didn't argue with her on the issue. It was a no win situation with Doris.

Jonas grabbed the number off the desk and wrote it down. "Leave that girl alone, something about her ain't right son." She whispered to him.

Jonas nods his head, yes. As if he was going to take heed to the advice, but he had other plans for the sexy nurse.

Tia gave Doris a kiss and they walked out of the room.

Chapter 15

Bobby made it out of the hospital, within a week like the doctors had expected. He spent every waking moment planning, strategizing and in deep thought, while laid up in the hospital bed. He wanted revenge and didn't care who had to die in order to achieve it.

While on vacation, as he called it, a lot of the Bogus Boyz came to visit and pay their respect to their unofficial leader. Bobby loved and craved the attention, even though he earned it through hard work, determination and the will to kill. Bobby was a gangster by all means. He established this fact early in life. While, Omar busied himself chasing money, Bobby hung around stone cold killers. His early mentors were Ram and Baldie. The two goons, who made history in Chicago by killing two DEA Agents, their rep was unheard of. They were sentenced to death row, in the federal system. If bobby wasn't so young at the time he would've been right there at the time of the murders.

Omar paced the room as bobby relaxed on his couch, his right leg had a cast on it and his arm was bandaged up. The bullet from Bolo's automatic rifle was powerful, but lucky for bobby it went through some flesh in his legs and kept going. Otherwise, the sniper like bullet would have damaged his leg forever. All in all, he was lucky to still be alive and be able to walk again.

Bobby's leg healed properly. The month long stay in the hospital did justice for his wounds. He was set to get the cast off in another week or two.

A black Uzi rested beside Bobby's propped up leg on the couch. The machine gun was within arms reach.

"Omar, why you so paranoid?"

He stopped in mid-stride. "Look I followed ya lead on this one. The little amateurs of yours missed Nia. Now, all hell is going to break loose."

"I got this, O. I told you soon as I get this cast off I'm going straight at them...We going to kill Nia, Jonas and whoever else wants to get in our way of taking Hustlers Row from the Blackout Gang." Bobby said, with authority.

Bobby was smart, even though Omar relished in the money and fame, Bobby thought he was the smartest brother. Bobby didn't care about hustler's row. He just needed to engage Omar's attention. Bobby knew that Omar's only god was money. He figured it be best to give his brother some incentive to help him defeat the Blackout Gang and he could get all the money and help he needed to get them out of the way. While, Omar paid for it. War didn't come cheap and the side that had deeper pockets, almost always won.

"Rico and Doc hit Black Smoke today, but they caught Rico with a dome shot. What the fuck is these little rug rats doing? I might need to hire some professional help." Omar said and then started to pace again.

"I told Jonas that I wanted a meeting with him a week ago. Now, since Rico got hit on their territory, he knew that the Bogus Boyz had something to do with it."

"He know your not affiliated. You still could meet with him." Bobby's eyes beamed at the thought. He could kill Jonas and then concentrate on Nia.

"I'm not going to meet him now."

Bobby just laughed at his brother's weakness, but he wanted to seize the moment. "Listen, Jonas is the real deal, but Nia is what keeps him strong. We set up a meeting with the both of them and kill two stones in one try."

"Bobby, that's stupid." Omar said.

He stopped and plopped down on the other end of the sofa. "You're a war veteran. You know the element of surprise is the key to winning. Shit, you got more murders then I got enough money to fight the cases." Omar just shook his head at Bobby's stupid suggestion.

Bobby gave Omar a hard stare. He wanted to kill Omar for calling him stupid. If he wasn't my brother, was all he thought.

Omar pointed to a bag lying underneath the glass table. It was a couple of inches away from Bobby's reach.

"It's a hundred thousand in there. Lay low for another month or two, while I do some damage control. We done need nobody knowing that your home. I can meet Jonas, make an excuse about Rico and then free lancing and try to gain some trust, so that we can have a better angle with the situation."

"That nigga is a snake, and I should've killed his ass a long time ago."

Bobby grabbed the Uzi and placed it on his lap. He was done talking. Bobby wanted to go home and plan for the next hit.

"Man look! I'm...We getting to much money for this. Murder's Row is clearing a lot of money. I got ya whole damn gang pushing the work."

"No, I got my boys pushing the work. You just supply me, but that's my turf."

Bobby made it clear to Omar. He understood though, that had been the plan for years.

"So, why jeopardize that...We can take Hustlers Row in the long run and without so much violence."

"I always knew you were soft as shit, but you was my brother. That's why I always protected you from the wolves." Bobby said, before being cutt off by Omar.

"I'm not trying to hear none of that shit. I'm the one who always had to bail your ass out of trouble, so listen for a god damned second."

"Nigga are you backing my play or what! I told you I don't got time for this scary shit."

Bobby grew tired of trying to play mind games with Omar. Either, he was riding or not. It wasn't any in betweens. Bobby knew how they played. Jonas was coming to get all of them, once he found out that they killed Black Smoke and tried to hit Nia. There wasn't going to be no talking, meeting or alliances formed now. It was do or die and Bobby planned to do. There wasn't no turning back now. The killing already started and the drama was in the air... The war was on.

Chapter 16

Jonas spent the better part of the day with Tia. He took her shopping, they went and played some video games and caught an early movie at the theatre.

Joey, slamming his foot to the floor, brought the Paddy Caddy to a halt just in the nick of time. Thumping his hands on the dashboard, he screamed out, "Why did the cowardly bastard have to do that? I wanted to nail him!"

After the movie, Jonas went and dropped Tia off past Lisa's salon. Their day had been fun. He felt like he was making strides, building a relationship with his daughter.

He headed straight home, after he left the salon, Jonas wanted to freshen up, after the long day of fun and games with his daughter. He didn't have any plans for the night. Though, he thought about calling up Diamond Dre and Smoke, to see what they had planned for the night. Maybe, he could hang out with the crew tonight. It had been awhile since the murders occurred in front of the club. So, he figured there wasn't any heat on the gang, at this time.

Jonas walked out of the bathroom with just his towel wrapped around his waist. He had a nice chiseled frame from the constant sit-ups, push-ups and running during his incarceration.

He headed straight to the kitchen. "Ring, ring, ring, ring." His phone went off right before he opened the cabinet.

Jonas turned and went into the living room. His cell phone sat face up on the glass table. "Ring, ring, ring, ring."

"Yo!" Jonas answered in a calm tone.

"Do you recognize my voice?" A female voice asked.

"How could I ever forget?"

"Don't say my name." She said.

There was an awkward silence for a second, before she continued.

"They just tried to kill Nia early this morning. I been checking, but I don't think she checked into any hospital, so she must be good."

Jonas stood there in silence trying to register the information.

"Jonas?" She said.

"Yeah, I'm here."

"You alright?"

"I'm straight. Who's behind this?"

He needed to know who was behind this act of disrespect and wanted answers, he also knew blood had to be spilled. An example must be set. Chicago would expect one, if nobody else in the B.O.G did. Nia was a board member. This was the second attempt on her life. Jonas couldn't just let this one slide by. Chicago was watching.

"Also, Smoke was killed on 66th and Justine. What's going on Jonas? You owe me, at least that. Remember, I'm a friend."

"I'm not sure myself." Jonas said.

"Well, we don't either."

"I need you to get me any information you have on this stuff." Jonas said.

"I'll try."

"Please." Jonas replied.

"I'll try. I got to go. I'll talk to you later and my sister said hi. She's mad you haven't been by to see us."

"We'll get together soon. You know it's still too early."

"I know. I'll see you later." She said, with concern in her voice.

Then the phone went dead. Jonas stood there enraged. He knew who pulled such a dangerous move off. It had to be no one other than Bobby. He was the only one with the balls to try and kill Nia, then hit Smoke on B.O.G's block. It was one of his signature moves. Bobby pulled the move off twice before and it proved to be successful for him.

He quickly dialed a number. "Diamond D get the team together and meet me out in Oaklawn."

"Man, the city in an uproar. We been trying to holla at you all day."

"I forgot and left my phone in the spot. I was with Tia today." Jonas replied.

"I just spoke with Nia, she straight."

Those last words relieved Jonas. The uncertainty of Nia being hit had been eating him up inside. He moved over towards the midnight grey couch. Jonas dropped into the soft and sunk into the comfy leather couch. He laid back and propped his feet up on the circular glass table, and grabbed a black leather pillow and sat it on his lap.

"Was she hit?" He still had to confirm Dre's answer.

"Nah, they put a show on."

Jonas already knew who they were. "Make sure she makes the trip."

"Aight."

He disconnected the line and tossed both the pillow and phone down beside him. Jonas leaped up and headed towards the room.

The facts had become clear. They were no longer the predators, instead they were now the prey being hunted. He understood what needed to be done. It was time. The B.O.G needed to take back their authority, and ducking beef wasn't the way to do it. The gangs were built off of strength, obstinacy and dominance. One, who was willing to show courage at times of confusion and disorder, Jonas decided it was time to be the leader that he perceived himself as. It was time for action.

Chapter 17

A light drizzle descended down on the quiet street. Thick rain clouds formed in the air, giving the skies a dark gray look. Night was rapidly approaching, but some rays of light still tried to sneak a peek through the clouds.

Traffic on 67th and Marquette was light, but still flowed accordingly on this Friday evening. Store's remained open, but none entered or exited the establishments.

A forest green, Cadillac Escalade pulled up slowly to the red light on 67th and Racine. The driver looked both ways and made a right hand turn onto Racine. A marked police cruiser sat in the lot of Mimi's BBQ place.

"Shit!" Marcus said. He continued driving at a nice pace. The cruiser got behind the Escalade, flipping on its flashing lights. Marcus glanced at the rearview. He shook his head for the stupid mistake of making the illegal right.

Marcus was from Englewood. He drove for Ken-Ken personally. Marcus moved the product from spot-to-spot and also picked up all the major deliveries for Ken-Ken. He didn't take part in any other activity than this. Ken-Ken made sure he kept Marcus on the low and away from the other gang activities. He was too important for the other frivolous things. At any given time, Marcus could be transporting twenty kilograms of cocaine or a couple kilograms of Heroin across the city.

Marcus pulled over to the curb and slammed his fist on the steering wheel in frustration. Through all his trips, he never once got pulled over, but also he never took an illegal right when he was driving dirty. His phone went off immediately once he pulled over.

Ken-Ken always made it a habit to follow Marcus, a few cars behind. He saw the stupid mistake he made and cursed under his breath when he done it.

Marcus grabbed the phone and answered. "Yo!"

"What the fuck you do that for?" Ken-Ken asked furiously.

"My bad...We good though. I'm going to handle this."

"I hope so! I'm at the end of the street, if you need me."

"Aight."

Ken ended the phone call. He pulled the navy blue, Jeep Cherokee over behind a car that offered him a good vantage point to watch what was going on. The raido picked up and started beating hard on the jeep. Ken sat there contemplated his next move. Marcus had fifty kilograms of cocaine in the SUV and two kilograms of Heroin. Ken had just snatched the drugs from his stash spot. He had intended to pass them out to the other B.O.G. members.

The Officer turned the sirens off and kept the lights flashing. He stepped out of the cruiser wearing a rain coat with a hood covering his head, rain beaded and pooled at the top of his hood before rolling down the sides and his hand rested on the top of his gun hanging in its holster.

He stepped, slowly, to the Escalade. The Officer stopped a few feet in back of the SUV and glanced in the tinted back window. He then proceeded, cautiously, to the driver side door.

The Escalade window came down, quickly, as the Officer approached. Smoke, slightly, flowed out of the vehicle. Marcus had fired a cigarette up. He was nervous, He had to think fast. Chicago Police Department was known to disregard the rules a lot of times. They pulled people over and illegally searched their vehicles. Even when no reasonable suspicion existed, and even went as far as planting drugs on known gang members that they wanted off the streets.

Several other cruisers arrived on the scene. One cruiser parked in front of the Escalade. Making any attempt for an escape fruitless. The other cruiser pulled directly on the driver side of the Escalade.

"Out of the vehicle and keep your hands where I can see them." The Officer said, with his gun drawn on Marcus. The cigarette hung, slightly off his lip while he kept his hands in the air. "I got my license and insurance in the glove. Ain't no need to go through all of this."

"Get your ass out that vehicle before I think your not complying with a law enforcement officer, trust me boy... you don't want to get on my bad side, not a good side to be on if you get my drift."

Chicago PD was known for killing innocent black youth with no intention on harming the officers. Marcus knew the routine. Now, he had to make a decision. Comply and go to jail, or resist and risk getting killed. The Officer didn't give him time to think; he grabbed the door and snatched Marcus out of the SUV with his left hand. Marcus landed hard on the wet ground. He snatched Marcus up off the ground like a rag doll and shoved him against the Escalade. The two other Officers just watched from their vehicles. The officer's knew how 'psycho' Mike was. The other two didn't want any part of the action.

Mike cuffed Marcus and secured him in the backseat of his cruiser. The Escalade driver's door remained open, while Mike went and opened the rest of the SUV doors, in order to check the vehicle.

Officer Mike had earned the reputation as "Psycho Mike" and was notorious on the streets for this type of illegal behavior. He hated gang members, and thought that every black youth belonged to one. He wanted them all off of the streets of Chicago. Along with his hate for blacks, Mike also had a gambling problem. He lost more than he won. Mike loved to bet on the college games. Weather, they were basketball or football. With his habit of losing, Mike resorted to pulling over the young blacks that drove expensive cars or trucks. Mike knew he could get some spare change, drugs or anything of value that he could pawn, to come up with some gambling money.

"Stupid bitch!" Ken-Ken yelled. He was pissed. Marcus had failed once again to follow through with the plan. He had explained, clearly, to Marcus the procedures of what he should do if he ever got pulled over. Ken-Ken wanted to pull off, but couldn't. He needed to see, if they were going to find the drugs.

Mike searched the front of the vehicle first. It was spanking clean inside the wood grain steering wheel and frame out lining the radio and other features of the SUV gleamed. Mike headed to the backseat. He reached under, and founded a couple duffle bags. He smiled to himself. Mije had been on the force for ten years now and knew how drugs were transported throughout the city. He snatched one bag from under the seat, and placed it on the leather seat. Psycho Mike opened the bag, and twenty kilograms of cocaine appeared wrapped in plastic. He quickly took four out and left them on the seats. Mike snatched the remaining two bags out from under the seat. He gathered heavy bags up and took them back to his cruiser.

"Shit! Shit!" Ken-Ken yelled out loud in frustration. He reached underneath the seat and grabbed Kel-Tec, which held fifty shots. The semi-automatic was loaded to the top. Ken-Ken sat the heavy machine on his lap. He contemplated running up on the Officer and taking the drugs back.

"Shit, it's not even paid for yet." Ken-Ken blurted out loud.

Psycho Mike sat the duffle bags on the front seat. He hurried back to the Escalade and grabbed the four other kilograms. Mike tucked them under his coat, so the heavy down pour wouldn't damage anything. He strolled over to the officer that was closer to him. Psycho Mike hopped in the cruiser and sat the four kilo's on the ground. "Go ahead and put these up for us."

"Okay Mike." The officer replied.

Psycho Mike hopped out of the vehicle and headed back to his cruiser. He pulled back his hood. Then turned to speak to Marcus. Mike reached back and slide the plastic screen across.

"I didn't find any license in the truck, but I found three bags of drugs. Now, we could end this right here. I'll call my friend on the task force and you cooperate. Maybe, he'll even let you walk, if you tell him who you work for or where you got these drugs. Or I just book you on the drugs and tell them not to work with you."

Marcus started sweating in the backseat. He was twenty-one years old and never been in trouble in his life. Jail wasn't even in his mind.

"What would you do, if I tell you right now who drugs they were? Would I still get arrested?"

"No, I'll tell them you cooperated with me." Mike said.

"My partner is parked in the blue jeep back there... don't look plus he has a gun."

"Alright, you better be correct because if you're lying to me, I'm going to give you a real old fashion Chicago PD ass whipping."

"Hurry up; he might be calling for backup to help get the drugs back." Marcus said, scared. He knew the plan Ken-Ken had put in effect. The B.O.G would be there in a matter of minutes, after Ken-Ken made the call.

Psycho Mike grabbed his walkie. "Hey Fred, blue Jeep, parked in the back of me. The suspect says he has a gun, and is his partner. Spin around the corner from the back, and I'll take him from the front."

"Roger that!"

The cruiser that was parked in front of the Escalade pulled off. Fred rode down the street, slowly. He glanced at

Ken-Ken on the phone, though he could barely see inside the jeep from the fogged up windows.

Ken-Ken slouched down in the seat when the cruiser started approaching. He still held the phone to his ear. Ken-Ken contemplated making the call. He had hoped this very moment never occurred, but it did. Now, he had to decide. Ken-Ken griped the semi-automatic weapon firmly with his finger resting on top of the trigger.

"Aye, I'm going to call you back. I'll see when you get here." Ken-Ken disconnected the line, and threw the phone across the seat. He took his eye off the cruiser that was in front of him for one second. Ken-Ken saw the cruiser make a left and disappear, as he glanced out the rearview mirror. He figured now was the time. Ken-Ken couldn't just let fifty-two kilograms be taken so easily. Psycho Mike took their merchandise without a fight and he knew that the Board Members wouldn't accept this, by no means, it made them look weak.

Ken-Ken reached back into the jeep and grabbed an umbrella. He stepped out of the vehicle, concealing the gun and opened the umbrella. Ken-Ken was dressed in denim jeans, and a black t-shirt with the LV design on the front, that stood for Louis Vuitton. He stepped onto the side-walk.

Psycho Mike eyed Ken-Ken the whole way in his rearview mirror. He was prepared for the assault. He grabbed his, police issued, Glock. As he was doing this, the police cruiser crept back up the street. Psycho Mike seen his fellow officer from afar in the mirror.

"The guy with the umbrella!" he yelled into the walkie-talkie.

Psycho Mike leaped out of the cruiser with his gun, drawn high in the air, towards Ken-Ken. He raced over to the side walk in front of him.

Ken-Ken froze in mid-stride. "Bitch nigga!" He mumbled to himself. He knew Marcus had told them about the plan. Ken-Ken didn't care though. He planned on getting those drugs back.

Fred trotted towards ken-ken from his backside. He was just six feet away from ken-ken when he froze. "Hands in the air! Hands in the air!"

Ken-Ken stood there and dropped the umbrella. Fred pounced on him with force. Psycho Mike ran over and helped detain Ken-Ken. They quickly searched him, while the rain fell hard. A weapon was found, and he was placed in the cruiser with Fred. He got behind the wheel of his patrol car and sped off to the police station.

Chapter 18

A lamp sat in the corner of the living room. It shined brightly, giving off much needed light. Other than the lamp, nothing else decorated the home. The walls were freshly painted and mini-blinds provided privacy from the outside world.

The group sat around in plastic lawn chairs. Jonas, Bolo, Flip Toney, Nia, Trina and Diamond Dre were all in a circle in the middle of the room. The place was Diamond's but he had yet to furnish the house. So, for the time being they designated it as a meeting place for the B.O.G. The group was trying to be discreet about their meetings. Especially, Jonas, so the suburbs of Oak Lawn seemed appropriate for him.

Jonas was slouched back, and stoned from smoking some high quality bud. A million thoughts ran through his head. The crew had remained quiet and let Jonas do the talking, although they had voting rights and say so in any matter dealing with the gang. Jonas had been mad, frustrated and upset about the loss of Black Smoke, it hit him hard. He couldn't understand how the B.O.G's soldiers let somebody come up in their strong hold, and blow Smoke's brains out, in broad daylight. The act was unheard of and impossible, so he had thought. They had a gunner on the roof and numerous youths roaming the streets with guns. Jonas tried to pin the blame on one of the other five Board

Members, but he couldn't It wouldn't be right. It was Black Smoke's responsibility to have the place secure. Nia had never let that happen on her watch. He thought, quietly, to himself. Jonas had to make a decision though.

"I want y'all to go round up everybody that was on the Row this morning, and who ever had a gun on them! They are getting violated."

Trina leaned forward out of the chair, her face grave and said, "What's the penalty?"

"They owe us a mission, and not just any mission, Smoke got murdered because of their bullshit. They owe us a homie!"

"I understand what you mean." Trina said.

Jonas didn't have to tell her what he wanted from them. One of his best friends was murdered. They had to be held responsible for his death.

Jonas rubbed his face. The room was quiet except for the sound of rain drops hitting the window at a rapid pace. He stopped, and stared at his members. Jonas knew what they wanted to hear. Everybody wanted blood. Bobby and the Bogus Boyz had violated their trust. An example needed to be sent.

"We going to hit bobby hard now." Jonas said, before being cut off by Nia.

"We been talking about what needs to be done, let's just get the shit done...I'm sick of all this talking!" Nia screamed out of frustration.

She was nearly murdered; her agitated emotions spoke for her. Jonas gave her an evil stare. He understood how frustrated she was, but her outburst was disrespectful, especially towards him, their leader.

"You need to calm down and listen." Jonas said through clenched teeth.

The old Jonas would've leaped up and smacked some sense into his sister, but Jonas knew better. Those long years had taught him a valuable lesson about patience. About thinking without your emotions clouding your judgment, and looking at the bigger picture. Jonas knew murder was necessary in the culture. How else would you be able to bring peace to people that were immune to murder.

These very people saw murder as nothing. They had been watching it happen all of their lives. Weather, they participated in it or not. It was a part of life in Chicago. Just like any other place in America. But they respected it. Murders were a sign of power, the more a city or neighborhood had the more fear and respect they gained, regardless of their motive, the end result was always the same. But, Jonas knew murder wasn't always necessary on every occasion. Nia didn't understand any of his logic. She ruled by instilling fear in enemies. By forcing them to do as she said, and murdering anybody that got in her way.

"Jonas, they tried to kill us today!" Nia shook her head, and leaned back in the chair. She was vexed.

Jonas loved his sister, but he knew she could be off balanced at times. She held the B.O.G down for years and ruled in her own way, but her way was sure to get the crew, either killed or imprisoned.

"I think we need to relax and get on the same page." Trina said.

Everybody nodded their heads in agreement.

"Listen, this is who we should hit now Joey, Omar and Bobby."

"I agree with you, but why Joey? He's still a kid." Jonas asked, although he knew the answer. He needed to see Nia's logic behind it. Joey was in the gang now, and his basketball dreams were long gone. So, if Bobby and Omar were killed, he would surely want revenge for their deaths.

"Joey's a Bogus Boy!" Nia said, and leaned forward. She placed both of her elbows on her knees. Nia was still dressed as earlier with her tight shorts on and all. "Omar is financing all of this shit, and if he's out of the way, then the money dries up and we can crush all of them."

Jonas gave a slight smile to himself. He liked Nia's aggression. He just needed to tame her at times.

"Where's Ken-Ken? He ever gets back from making that run?"

"He was suppose to been back. I waited out at the spot for hours on him." Flip Toney said.

He reached into his black jeans and pulled a phone out. He dialed Ken-Ken's number, but it went straight to voice mail.

"What's the plan?" Nia asked looking towards Jonas. He was deep in thought, while gazing at Flip.

Jonas stood up and walked across the hardwood floor. He stopped a couple feet from the group and turned to address them.

"I want y'all to personally go send a message to them niggas over on Murder's Row. Nia you lead the squad. I only want my best three on this." He glanced at Trina, then to Bolo who had a distant look in his face, as if he wasn't even in the room. Bolo heard Jonas's remark and snapped out of his daze. He nodded at the instructions Jonas gave.

"We don't need any of the little homies fucking nothing up. For now on, I want only y'all doing the work, until I reach out to one of my partners back in Joliet." Jonas Said.

Flip Toney tried to call Ken-Ken again. Trina relaxed in the chair. She was curious about what Jonas said. "Who ya partner?" Trina asked in a concerned tone.

She had a right to be concerned. Outsiders weren't allowed to know the inner workings of the B.O.G's war activities, especially when it dealt with making hits.

"Amir!"

"Oh yeah, the one from Chester." Nia said.

"Where?" asked Trina.

"It's right outside of Philly." Nia said and then glanced over at Jonas. She wanted him to break the news to the group.

"Yeah, I made a vow to my man back in the joint. We helped each other out through some of the roughest years in Joliet, so in return for his loyalty I gave him a piece of the B.O.G... Sorta like an unofficial board member." He looked around the room. "I did it because he gave me access to his crew."

Amir was doing multiple life sentences in Joliet for killing a witness that had fled to Chicago. He was part of a group called the "Young Gunz" Amir came from a neighborhood in Chester named Killa Hill. He killed, robbed and sold plenty of cocaine on the streets. Amir mostly got his money in Delaware. Where, he had a lot of connections with the Muslims, and some serious goons that killed for a living.

Nieem, who was Amir's cousin from Killa Hill, Needed a witness in a case to disappear. Their cousin named, Lil Nigga, had murdered two people in cold blood and got arrested, then charged with a double homicide. He faced the death penalty. The witness had been a close friend of the group. Once, Lil Nigga was arrested, the witness fled to Chicago to hide out until it was time to testify against him in court. Nieem got word of his whereabouts and asked Amir to take the trip out to Chicago. He accepted the request. He was extremely loyal to the family. Nieem sent two youngsters with Amir to watch his back and for reinsurance in case things went south.

He found the witness on a deserted street, so he had thought and murdered him right there in cold blood. Amir fled the scene, but got pulled over by the Chicago Police.

The driver got scared, and wanted to pull over. After, Amir told him that he was going to bust a cap in the cop. The driver froze briefly, then stomped the gas and took the police on a pursuit that that ended quickly. The police had rammed the back of the car while it was turning a corner. The driver lost control of the vehicle and crashed into a parked car. The driver was flung through the front window from the force of the impact. The air bags inflated with such pressure, t it knocked the passenger out cold when it made contact with his head. The passenger was left in a vegetable state. Amir had lost his grip on the gun and was trapped in the crushed vehicle. He along with the passenger was arrested with the smoking gun. The driver died at the scene.

Amir arrived at Joliet two years later. He ran into a couple of problems with the different gangs running around in the prison, and that's when he meant Jonas. He made Amir's stay easy in Joliet. They became friends instantly, and plotted ways to make money.

Jonas went and took his seat." Anybody got a problem with that?" He asked in a business like manner. Jonas wanted the trust of his crew. He needed them to understand that his friendship with Amir's crew was valuable.

"Nah." said Trina.

"I'm only going to use them when it's necessary. They're good and loyal Muslims. They sell drugs, and kill but they value trust and friendship. I've talked to Amir's cousin, Nieem, plenty of times. He's a good man. I gave him my word that I would look out for Amir in Joliet, and I did just that. So, it's nothing that he wouldn't help me with for that single favor I did for his family."

Nia knew the story well. She hadn't met Nieem, but she knew how Jonas felt about the two out-of-towners.

"Aight, so what is up with Bobby and Omar bitch ass?" Nia said, trying to get back on topic.

"Soon, as we find them or where they lay, y'all got the green light. I just don't want no wild cowboy shit when it comes to these two." Jonas said, locking eyes with Nia trying to get the message across.

She was delighted to hear the words. "Good, I got somebody sitting on Joey now. I want to wait, though. He could lead us to his brothers."

Jonas nodded. He was happy to see that Nia was thinking for once.

"I got word that Bobby is hiding in the Wild 100's." Flip said.

Everybody glanced at him. Flip was a money maker, not a gun slinger. He surprised everybody with his remark and he saw their reaction. "He got to be held responsible for Smoke." Flip shook his head. He hated how they caught Smoke slipping. Flip figured if it could happen to Smoke, it could happen to anybody. This whole beef was weighing heavy on him.

"Diamond, I need you to go check on Ken-Ken, see what's up? Take, Flip with you out to the spot, and go check his girl Shay spot too. I don't know, if he heard about all the shit that went down today."

They talked a little bit more about the beef, and about how their territories were doing. Jonas then ended the meeting.

Chapter 19

The night had been a long one for Ken-Ken, he slept inside a dingy cell with no windows, and on a steel, long, chair that was bolted to the wall. The room reeked of urine, and the water was stale it came out of a one-dimensional sink set that also had a toilet attached to it. He slept off and on and was lucky to have gotten a good hours rest. Unable to sleep that night, Ken-Ken paced the empty cell. He did this all the way until the following morning, when the shift changed.

Psycho Mike had failed to process, either, Ken-Ken or Marcus. He wanted the gang taskforce to see them first. The arrest was big and Mike couldn't predict how far this could go, so he placed both of them in separate, empty, cells in the police station for the night.

Ken-Ken sat in an old wooden chair. His left arm rested on the metal table, while the other lay across his lap. The room was completely empty with no windows. The walls were painted white, the paint was old and cracked, with flakes of paint revealing hints of gray under the surface, and large yellow stains from the lack of being cleaned. Two other wooden chairs sat forgotten across from the table. Ken-Ken had been brought to the interrogation room right after he was served breakfast, which consisted of a coffee and doughnut. It had been hours, now, that he sat inside the dingy room. He daydreamed, fell a sleep and even paced the room at times.

The metal door swung open. The Night Stalker strolled through the door wearing army fatigue pants, black Nike sneaker boots, and a black t-shirt with Gang Unit written across the front in bold white letters. A silver badge dangled from a chain down the middle of his chest. Nakira followed him into the room. She was dressed, simple, in a pair of black fatigue pants, same black t-shirt as the Night Stalker, and wore similar looking boots. Nakira moved to the side, and held the door for James Weinstein. He stepped into the room carrying a brown brief case in his right and held a white Styrofoam cup filled with coffee in his other. James had a confident demeanor about him. He stood straight up, showing casing his full height, and slim size. James Weinstein was all business. He wore a black suit, a white dress shirt underneath and a yellow silk tie to compliment his looks.

James was a District Attorney on the state level, who prosecuted only cases that were from the gang unit. He put hundreds of gang members behind bars in Chicago, and had secured three death penalty victories before Governor Ryan ordered a moratorium on executions, and death qualified cases. James Weinstein reigned supreme in the courtroom. He held a 90% conviction rate, and was known to go the extra mile and do to whatever it took to secure a conviction.

Nakira closed the door and leaned up against it. She crossed her arms and holding them loosely across her chest. While, the Night Stalker and James took a seat in the chairs, James put his briefcase on the concrete floor next to him and sat his cup down on the table. He leaned back and crossed his legs. The whole crew had aloof expressions on their faces. They came for answers.

Ken-Ken slouched in the chair and tried to gauge the people's demeanor. He couldn't, though. They were professionals. Although, the act looked scripted, it wasn't. They came into contact with criminals on a daily basis, so they were good at their profession.

"Ken-Ken, what's up?" The Night Stalker said, leveling his gaze on Ken-Ken. "We confiscated Forty-six kilos from your SUV, and you were armed with a deadly firearm."

"That's an easy thirty years in the Federal system, if we choose to let them have it." James said. The prosecutor's pale face showed sever lack of sunlight if not for the lack of pink eyes, he could have easily passed as albino and he either had the best poker face in the world or he was dead serious.

"Now, if you're willing to help, then I can talk Ol' Mr. Weinstein over here into keeping the case on the state level, but we want the Blackout Gang." Said Night Stalker looking like a grinning idiot.

Ken-Ken was caught of guard, and his body language showed it. "Blackout Gang!" He said with a dumbfounded look.

"Yeah, the gang you belong too. Look, we don't got time to be bullshitting with you. We know you're a board member, and Jonas's right handed man, with the drugs that is."

Nakira's face expression changed. She was surprised she didn't know who Ken-Ken was, or if he was part of the gang. The Night Stalker failed to inform her of this revelation. He was holding back information from her. This had to stop, immediately, if she planned on rising in the ranks. Nakira stood straight up, and paid close attention to Ken-Ken's words.

"I can guarantee that nobody will know about your arrest yesterday, I'll get you protection once this thing goes to trial, and you'll get a piece of all their assets we're going to forfeit from them," said James.

"All we want is the Blackout Gang!"

Ken-Ken sat there with a dumbfound look plastered on his face. They were guaranteeing freedom with money to boot. All he had to do was sell his members out. It seemed unreal to him. "I don't know." He folded his arms across his chest, and the thought of cooperating dashed across his mind. Ken-Ken knows the rules, well. Snitches were treated like scum in the streets of Chicago, just like any other place in America's streets. Ken-Ken knew he wouldn't be able to be seen in his beloved city ever again, if he went through with this. He loved Chicago especially, his neighborhood of Englewood. He shook his head, no.

"Look, don't think I won't march over to the United States District Attorney's Office. They would love to get their hands on somebody like you." James uncrossed his legs and leaned forward across the table. "And when they get you... you, best believe you'll be doing jail time, then. No matter, if you cooperate or not." He finished and leaned back into the uncomfortable seat.

The Night Stalker rubbed his right hand through his curly black hair. He was slightly tanned from his beach trip over the weekend with his family. His forearms were massive from his constant exercising, and were extremely hairy. He slammed his large hand down on the metal desk. James looked at him startled, but he kept his cool. James knew how crazy he could get at times. The two worked hundreds of cases together.

"Stop playing fucking games!"

"Aye, give me some time to think. I've known these people all my life. I just can't give them up like that." Ken-Ken tried to explain. He knew that he was finished, now with Marcus telling on him. Forty-six kilo's, which was supposed to be fifty, now was being attributed to him. Let alone the firearm. It was going to be a long time before Ken-Ken ever set foot on the streets of Chicago again. He needed to get in touch with Jonas. Ken-Ken thought to himself.

Nakira started pacing the floor. She never turned her gaze away from Ken-Ken. She was upset. It was like a continuing cycle in Chicago. A black man gets caught red handed with drugs or guns. They get arrested, interrogated, and immediately turn snitch. This sorta culture was tearing the black communities apart in America. She hated being a part of it, but this was her job. Nakira didn't sign up for this part, though. Yes, she wanted to help clean-up the city of Chicago from all the gang violence, but not like this. A man was supposed to stand up, and take his own weight. At least that's what her brothers, uncles and cousins from Englewood taught her. She realized though that throughout the years, the rules began to change. Thugs cooperating with the authorities were rising to the level of being an epidemic. The snitch culture was tearing families apart, and at the age of thirty-five she was watching it firsthand. All with the help of people like James Weinstein, and Patrick Saw-aka-

"The Night Stalker" Nakira was disgusted looking at the two Caucasian men trying to break another black family apart. She buried her feelings though. In order to break the cycle, she had to be a part of the process.

"Who do y'all what?" asked Ken-Ken.

The Night stalker snapped, "The Blackout Gang!"

The stars were shining extremely bright. A light breeze cooled down the otherwise humid night. School was finally out for the summer, so the night life in the neighborhood of 57th and Green St. was alive. Adults sat on their front porches drinking and smoking, whether it was marijuana or cigarettes, but they were just enjoying the beautiful night, while hustler's roamed the streets. This was the Bogus Boyz strong hold. They sold lots of china white out of the residential area. Due to the rawness of the heroin, and the murders that followed from the hot shots and turf wars, everybody dubbed the place Murder's Row. Omar supplied the area, but Bobby ran it with an iron fist. He fought his battles to keep it, and even murdered foes to stay far away from it.

Trina pushed the stolen caravan down 57th street. She slowed down, and turned onto Morgan. She was silent and in deep thought thinking about her brother. She thrived off the beauty of killing. Not that killing was beautiful at all, but she loved it.

Bolo relaxed on the passenger side. A skin tight black t-shirt covered his massive chest, and he clutched a Chinese made SKS assault rifle. The rifle's barrel was pointed toward the floor, while the butt of the rifle laid on his black fatigue pants. Nia sat right behind him. She also was dressed in black, and clutching a SKS.

Trina pulled over on 57th and Peoria. She wore similar gear, as Bolo and Nia. Trina parked and turned to look at Nia. "Aye, we're going to walk over to the next street."

"Trina, you don't have to come." Bolo said. He had murder in his eyes. Bolo had been thinking about Smoke all day. He missed his friend.

"Nah, I'm not missing out on this one." She didn't wait for him to respond back. She scooted the little arm rest up and hunched over to grab the AR15 concealed under Nia's seat.

Bolo scanned the street. Peoria was a quiet strip that no one hung out at, including gangs. Small homes occupied the street. Some had lights still on, others were abandoned, and some were just plain vacant. Nia had studied the street earlier in the day. She came up with the idea that this was the perfect street.

"Y'all ready?" asked Trina.

Nobody returned an answer. They hurried and got out of the van closing the doors softly behind them. The skilled killers didn't want to make a lot of noise. The group walked up the street, at a nice pace. Not to fast, and not to slow. Trina, as usual, kept her head continuously moving trying to familiarize herself with the area. Bogus Boyz controlled it, so she didn't want to be unprepared. They held the rifles close to their bodies, along side their legs, so nobody would notice, especially, the enemy.

Bolo saw the activity first. They quickly approached Green St. their was a bunch of "Bogus Boyz" members out on the street tonight. A couple teenage boys hung around a Cutlass Oldsmobile. One guy had, one foot out of the car with the other half of his body inside. Kanye West's verse on, 'I got what you need, was being played loud from the car, you could feel the thud of the base. The rest of the Bogus Boyz stood around bobbing their heads, while some across the street were serving two separate lines of fiends.

Nia whispered, "Hit everybody. We sending a message!" Then raised her SKS. She was only fifty feet away, and none of the Bogus Boyz bothered to look up at the three dressed in dark clothes. 'Bak, Bak, Bak, Bak, Bak, Bak!' Nia started gunning first. Trina followed suit. Bolo ran across the street, and fired on the crowd of fiends and gang members. Bogus Boyz and fiends scattered like roaches as they were interrupted by a tumult of hot lead.

Three boys fell immediately in front of the Oldsmobile. The others managed to duck and run for cover. Nia and Trina braced their selves, and aimed carefully while shooting at everything and anything that moved. They had been expecting return fire, but none came.

Trina lost her train of thought and dashed towards the car. Rat, inside of the Old's, was stretched across the chair trying to cover himself from the gunshots. A chrome .45 dangled in his right hand. Rat tried to look up, but Trina was on the side of the car. She riddled him with bullets. Trina stopped firing, and jumped over a couple of bodies. She was trying to make it over towards Bolo, where some of the Bogus Boyz were running up the street away from them.

On the porch, two men laid down trying to avoid being hit or seen by the assassins. They were supposedly on security, but froze in fear form the loud thundering of B.O.G's assault rifles. One man remained standing, though. He was determined to protect himself, or at least his friends who were running for safety. He held an AK 47 with a fifty shot banana clip hanging from it. Man-Man steadied the AK on Bolo and Trina. Seeing his chance, he started firing.

The loud sound caught Nia off guard. She was shooting to the right, across the street at the men sitting on the porch Nia glanced over her left shoulder, and saw the long flames erupting from the AK's barrel.

The bullets whizzed past Bolo, tearing into the car in front of him hard and loud. He ducked, and ran behind a parked car. Trina followed him. Man-Man had the two pinned down behind the car.

Nia raised the SKS, and unloaded on Man-Man; He got hit, immediately, in the chest, and stumbled backwards tumbling to the ground. Man-Man's head cracked open upon impact leaving a fresh pool of blood on the asphalt. The AK fell from his hands, and clanked on the ground along side of him.

"Come on! Come on!" Nia yelled at the top of her lungs.

The shooting ceased, and Nia was ready to go. Bolo peaked around the car, and jumped up when he saw Man-Man laid out on the ground face down. Trina rose up with her rifle held up and then ran behind Bolo.

Sirens were slightly heard in the distance. Nia made it to the van first. She hopped into the back of the van, breathing heavily from being out of breath. Trina hurried and slide behind the wheel, and Bolo made it to the passenger side. Everybody was breathing heavy from the block run. Trina started the engine, and peeled off. They made it safely out of the neighborhood. Trina pulled behind her Range Rover. The street was dark, and mostly abandoned buildings occupied the area.

BOOM!

Trina jumped at the sound of the assault rifle going off. Bolo brains were splattered across the passenger window. The windshield had cracked from the hole that the SKS's bullet made. Bolo slumped over. A big hole, the size of a tennis ball, leaked blood from the exit wound. Trina turned quickly, and looked at Nia.

"What the fuck?"

"He fucked up! Don't worry about it." Nia said.

Chapter 20

The drama had intensified on the streets, and Nia and Trina were at the far-front. It was shocking how the girls moved. With danger lurking behind every corner, they still remained calm and in control. By their actions, it often seemed like they were trying to prove a point. That's what some thought, especially due to the fact that they were women and beautiful women at that. But, it wasn't that. The girls just loved the lifestyle and money and murder were exciting, to them.

They went and dumped the van. Nia left Bolo's body in the vehicle and torched it. Everything she did was for a reason or to send a message. Trina knew this too, so she didn't second guess her partner about Bolo. Jonas might have even sanctioned it, so she thought. But, whatever the case was, Trina was standing by her sister.

Trina parked her all black Range Rover in front of the dilapidated house. It stood by itself, and an old worn down fence bordered the property, which separated the homes from each other on both sides. The grass was overgrown and littered with old bike parts, chip bags, trash bags filled with spoiled food and rodents like mice and rats roamed freely. The shades were drawn, but a soft glow shown through..

Nia stepped out of the truck, still wearing her all black gear from earlier, and Trina followed. Both scanned their surroundings. The street was quiet, and deserted. 63rd

Laflin didn't have too much action going on these days. Mostly drug addicts, squatters and runaways occupied the homes on the street. The homes were mostly abandoned, in disarray or section 8 residents that didn't keep up with the maintenance of the houses.

Trina pulled the rickety old storm door open, and entered. She stepped into the place with Nia on her heels. Trash was piled everywhere, and the place reeked of rot and decay, there had to be a dead animal buried amongst the clutter.

"Damn!" They said, at the same time holding their breath while walking on the little narrow trail leading to the kitchen, and basement. They quickly made their way to the basement stairwell. A dim yellow light illuminated their way from below. The steps creaked under their weight, as the two women crept downstairs. .

Two of the B.O.G's soldiers sat in plastic lawn chairs, and puffed on a fat blunt of weed. The walls and floor were made of solid concrete and the strong smell of marijuana and mold lingered in the air, the place was completely empty and unfurnished.

Nia stepped off the last step.

"Damn, I'm glad y'all down here smoking."

"We been firing up weed and cigarettes for hours to get that damn stinking smell out of here." J-Roc said.

He was in his early twenties, but been down with the Blackout gang since he was eleven. J-Roc was one of Nia's favorite goons. She liked the youngster because of his loyalty, bravery and the fact that he was a natural stone-cold killer.

He made his first kill at the age of sixteen, and attempted to kill a cop by the age of eighteen.

J-Roc held the Dutch in his hand and then inhaled it deeply, holding it in his lungs. He was dressed in a white t-shirt with 'Street Dreamz' in red lettering going across it, and a pair of denim shorts with some black Jordan sneakers.

"He tell y'all anything?" said Trina. She pointed to Joey, his face was battered and bloody. He was tied to a plastic chair, and shivering from being scared and naked. A small pool of his urine was pooled underneath the chair.

J-Roc and Pete had snatched Joey earlier that day. They had taken turns beating him relentlessly for hours. Joey's ribs on the right side were broken, and the bones in his right hand were shattered from his hand taking the blunt force of the metal bat, while trying to block being hit.

Pete took the Dutch from J-Roc. He had a black t-shirt on with 'RIP Black Smoke' in white letters, and wore some black jean shorts. Pete also wore a pair of Jordan's. He was one of Smoke's runners on Hustlers Row, and actually was out there the day he got murdered. Pete was young. He was only sixteen, but participated in numerous home invasions, and killed Latin Kingson on behalf of Smoke, before his passing. Pete remained famous in the younger Blackout group. All of the youngsters aspired to be like him, and rise up in the ranks.

Nia moved over to Joey and said, "Aye, where the fuck is Bobby?"

Joey raised his bloody head slightly. He was in extreme pain. He managed all the strength in his body to speak. "I don't know."

Trina snatched her forty calibers out from off her waist. She stepped closer to Joey, and smacked him with the side of the pistol.

"Where, the fuck is he!"

Joey couldn't respond. He tried to get his senses back. The pain was becoming unbearable. Trina pistol whipping him was nothing, he had become numb to pain at this point.

Nia saw that it was useless. Joey was too far gone to give any information. She blamed herself. Nia knew her and Trina should have tortured him themselves. "Aye, kill this bitch ass nigga." She glared at J-Roc.

Pete got up, and lifted the .45 that was lying in his lap.

"Nah, Pete, I said J-Roc."

J-Roc leaped straight up with a nine millimeter in his hand. The Dutch hung slightly off his lip. He hesitated for a moment, eyeing Joey and then squeezed the trigger. 'Boom! Boom! Joey's body jerked back in the chair and went limp.

"What'cha want me to do with the body?" He asked like it was nothing. A human being had just been murdered. Life meant nothing to him, or the rest of the people inside the basement.

Trina looked at Nia and then said, "Throw his punk ass at the top of 57th and Green, but wait until like four in the morning. Police probably still got it taped off right now."

"Aight." replied J-Roc, He took his seat, and continued smoking the marijuana.

Nia and Trina turned to leave. The night was still young, and they still had more to do. The two sexy ladies walked back up the creepy wooden stairs. J-Roc and Pete eyed them closely checking them out. When, they were finally out of sight Pete said, "Man I wish I could fuck Trina fine ass. I love her gangsta ass."

"Shut ya young ass up, and help me wrapped this stupid mutha fucka up."

Chapter 21

J onas drove in silence down the long dirt road. The backwoods of St. Charles, Illinois had beautiful scenery in the summer months, Long trees, green filled grass stretched far and wide, through the area.

Nia relaxed on the passenger side, as Jonas drove the Ford 350 up to a cabin. The place was secluded off the main road, and surrounded by tall Oak trees.

"Whose place is this?" Nia asked. She was confused why Jonas would want to come all the way out here just to talk with her. It didn't make sense. She had felt the vibe he gave her after she mentioned killing Bolo, and didn't like it at all.

"This was Bolo's hideout."

"Hide out for what?"

"In case we ever needed to lay-low from the Feds, enemies, or needed to plan some real dangerous shit in secret." He said, without even looking at her. "This is where he laid-low after he killed them witnesses for you in that triple homicide case." Jonas just stared at her, so the words could sink in her head.

Nia knew where Jonas was going with this. He wanted her to realize the stupid mistake she made. Let alone the blatant disrespect of his authority. Bolo was a trusted member and Jonas had total confidence in Bolo period. The two had come up through the system. They were "State raised", as some would call it.

Bolo loved Jonas like the brother he never had. Bolo came from a single mother home, and was his mother's only child. At the tender age of sixteen his mother died from a hot shot of heroin. Bolo was so distraught and sad, nothing mattered to him after that. He took revenge on his mother's death before killing the youngster who actually sold the dose to her. He got caught. Plead guilty to the murder and got sentenced to five to ten years of imprisonment with parole eligibility after five. During his time all he did was lift weights, read books of strategies of war and how to kill books with using just a knife. After two years into his sentence Jonas arrived at Joliet with him. It was just like old times for the two. Bolo hadn't seen Jonas since their Juvi days when they used to terrorize the other gangs and extort them for their food and money. They linked back up and grew a strong bond.

Bolo helped Jonas put the finishing touches on the structure of Blackout Gang. They made a pact in the joint that Bolo would be head of security and focus all his strength to maintain order in the crew, and on the streets. He did exactly that with an iron fist.

True to his word on being released early on parole, Bolo went out and linked up with Nia. She understood he was coming home with orders straight from Jonas to control the security aspect of Blackout Gang. Nia welcomed him with open arms.

Jonas pulled the truck up to the deserted cabin. The medium-size place was made out of Red Oak wood. A chimney stood erect at the top of the roof and only two windows could be seen from the dirty walk way. The two exited the vehicle.

"Jonas, why did we come all the way out here?"

"Cause I wanted to show you this place." Jonas glanced at the surrounding area. "Plus we needed a one-on-one. Shit been crazy lately and you been acting stupid."

"What the fuck is that supposed to mean?" Nia asked.

"It means that you're fucking up and I need to bring this shit to your attention."

"Oh, so now you checking me?"

Jonas just gazed at her. He walked off towards the front door. Nia was furious at his blatant disrespect; nobody ever challenged her authority that way.

"I don't got time for this shit." Nia mumbled to herself and strolled towards the door behind Jonas.

They walked into the place. A huge fireplace with wood stacked inside of it, laid at the back of the front room. A fluffy black and red sofa set decorated the floor. A 55" flat screen television hung up on the wall.

Nia walked in and looked around the place. She liked the color scheme and decor of the cabin. "I could've been bringing my baby here." She thought to herself. Nia tensed up when she seen Jonas go straight to the backroom without even saying a word. Nia eased her hand inside her Prada pocket book. She clutched a snub nose .357

Jonas came back carrying a big duffle bag. "Go ahead and sit down." He said, and threw the bag by her feet. "Put ya gun away too, I can't believe you would actually think I would harm you."

Nia was embarrassed, and ashamed that she even thought such a thing of Jonas. But she understood the streets. Nia came up hard in Chicago and Doris taught her well on how to survive by all means. Growing up the only girl, and with two brothers being gang members she had to adapt quickly to the abuse of them trying to make her tuff. Nia faced them head on. She fought back and gained their respect.

"I didn't have any gun clutched for you." Nia said, lying to Jonas.

"Yeah. Whatever." He said, and sat back on the sofa. "That's a million dollars in the bag." Jonas said with a straight face.

Nia eyes lit up. Besides Mark her lover, money and killing was her next love. Money brought so much pleasure to her dreams, and she killed to satisfy her hate for men.

"Nia why the hell did you kill my best friend? I mean you know how much Bolo meant to me and B.O.G. It was nothing that he wouldn't do to push the movement."

"Is that what this is all about?"

"That and the fact that you been acting like a damn crazy bitch. What the fuck is wrong with you? You making too many fucking stupid moves. You killing comrades without justification. You shooting out in the middle of fucking broad daylight, let alone the stupid club shooting you done."

"Jonas I been pushing the B.O.G for ten long years." Nia said.

"Yeah, I'm the fucking leader though." Jonas stood up. "I'm the fucking leader right? We agreed on this right?"

Nia just sat there with fire in her eyes. She always hated being told what to do. Especially from a man, but Jonas was the exception. She listened always to what he had to say and abided by it. Jonas word was law to her. But the money and numerous murders had her ego and pride in a chokehold. The reality of it, she knew Jonas was right.

"I'm the fucking Leader right?" Jonas stated.

"Jonas you been away for ten years. I'm the one who been putting food on the table. Making sure you was straight in the joint. Killing all the B.O.G enemies."

"Nia you wasn't doing shit until I supplied you with the connection. I got you the work to supply the blocks. I formed the alliances with the other gang heads!" Jonas said, with anger. "All from the fucking joint."

Jonas was right. Nia thought to herself. He was the one pulling all the resources together. She was just utilizing them and making sure he got his share of everything.

"What do you want me to say?" She asked with an attitude.

"Am I the fucking leader?" Jonas asked, then took a seat.

"Yes, Jonas you're the leader."

It was hard to defeat Nia in anything she tried her best to be strong at all times. She hated showing her weakness.

This quality of hers was achieved at a young age. Along with taking the usual whippings from her brothers, Nia had to deal with a real life crises. Juvi hall and Nia and Doris were the only ones at the house. Nia was sound asleep when she heard the door swing open and hit the wall hard. The noise made her jump up out of bed. She ran out of her room and stood at the top of the steps. A man wearing a long leather jacket had a knife to Doris neck, And the other hand over her mouth. Doris tried to struggle with the man. But due to her heavy drinking earlier it was no help, especially against two men. The other guy took his knife and cut the right leg of Doris pants. He jumped up when a noisy drink came to the doorway to see what all the commotion was. The door was slammed in his face.

Nia ran to her mother's room, and went into her tow drawer. On numerous occasions Nia had seen her mother's gun. Doris always eyed her, and told her that she would whip her ass until hell freezes over, if she ever touched the gun. Nia knew exactly what she meant. Doris beatings were harsh and long. Nia didn't want any parts of them.

She grabbed the small black .38 from underneath some of Doris's underwear. Nia ran down the small hall, and seen the man slipping Doris's panties off. She quietly walked down the steps. The guy with the leather coat looked up first. She aimed high and pulled the trigger. Nia hit the guy above his heart. She didn't even wait for him to drop before he fired at his friend. Nia let off two more shots. The mad fell directly on Doris. Blood was all over the door, and Doris's face and chest. Nia stood there amazed at the power of the small gun. Doris shook her out of the amazement. She took the gun from Nia and told her to run to her friend Mark's house. She took off without looking back.

Finally happy to hear her say yes, Jonas said, "Now the structure of B.O.G is what?"

"Please Jonas." Nia pleaded.

"The structure is what Nia?!"

"In order to kill a trusted member the whole commission has to vote on it."

"There wasn't a vote Nia. Now, you of all people knew the consequences."

"He fucked up Jonas. The hit was sloppy."

"You fucked up before too. How many witnesses did we have to pay? Let alone the one BOLO killed for you."

Nia dropped her head.

"Now this is the deal because I just did ten hard fucking years, and I'm not going back to jail."

Jonas got silent. Nia raised her head to see where Jonas was going with the violation. Death was the penalty, and she sure wasn't in the mood to die today.

"There's a million dollars in the bag. You can take it and go ahead out to Nevada with Mark, and relinquish your position of the board or you can keep your position but you have to promise the board that there would be no more unauthorized shootings. That you will come to the board first and consult with us and that you will accept your punishment."

Nia got nervous with the haste statement. She looked at Jonas with death in her eyes. "What's the punishment?"

"That for a full year you will donate a quarter of your profits to Bolo's young son's bank account and another quarter to out legal defense fund."

Nia stood up and paced the wooden floors her stilettos' clicked after every step. "Okay Jonas you win."

"Good! Now, you need to come out with a good story about why you killed Bolo...The homies is going to want an explanation." Jonas said.

"I could make some paperwork saying he was about to snitch." Nia was quick on her feet when it came to the street life. It was no doubt about it, Nia knew how to survive.

"You can't put that type of bone on Bolo, and expect it to fly...You got to do better than that."

Jonas hated the animal his sister became. He knew it all stemmed from when she first killed the two junkies trying to rape their mother, He was mad she was acting reckless, and she definitely deserved to be killed, but he loved his sister. Nia held him down all her life. So he couldn't order the ultimate punishment on her. Jonas would try his best to shield her. Bolo was his brother, but Nia was blood. And blood was thicker than water.

"I don't know any other angle besides Bolo was about to snitch." Nia said.

"Listen, I'ma put myself on the line for you on this one and say I ordered the hit, but next time you fuck up, we will bury you ass." Jonas said, with a coldness that shook Nia and it was hard to shake her.

"I'm going to get straight on top of it." Jonas said

Nia trotted back over to the seat and sat down; she was relieved Jonas promised to clean up her mess. Jonas sat back in a zone. Things were falling apart. Everything wasn't going according to his plan. If only I would've let Bobby Mackey vent my main man would be here and this war shit would not be. Jonas thought to himself. Nia pulled her phone out and dialed a number.

"Hey baby." Nia said.

"How are you doing?" Mark asked.

Nia let out a loud sigh. "I've seen better days."

"I seen Chicago all over the news."

"Yeah shit is crazy out here" Nia said.

After killing the two men that tried to rape Doris, Nia ran to her boyfriend Mark Thompson's house. Mark had been the only guy she ever slept with and was a sense of comfort for her. Mark was the only man that could ever capture Nia's heart. Although, she was ruff on the outside, Mark grasped her soft personality.

As she gained respect in the streets, Mark excelled in school. Mark graduated with honors from Penn State and took a job in Las Vegas selling high-end real estate for a brokerage firm.

Although they lived two different lives and he wanted her to walk away from the streets, he never imposed his will on her. With women flocking to him every which way, he always remained faithful.

Nia would often fly out to Vegas to gain a sense of peace when Chicago got crazy.

"I'm flying out there tonight, so arrange a private flight for me." Nia said.

"I'll handle that, as soon as we hang up."

"See if you can get a flight leaving from the St. Charles area."

"Okay" Mark said.

"How is the paperwork looking on the new spot out there?"

Mark had gained a significant foot hold in the real estate market in Nevada, so in return Nia started funneling her and Jonas's money through a Real Estate trust fund. He was the trustee on the fund, and the company was incorporated in Nevada. Where, secrecy of ownership was a top priory in the state.

"Things are better than I expected...We will go over things when you get out here." Mark said.

"Call me when you got the flight arranged." Nia said. Nia hung up the phone.

"Jonas I'm going out to Vegas for a few days."

Jonas always respected Mark. When Doris got arrested and charged with the two murders Mark and his family took care of Nia. Doris remained in custody for sex months until pleading guilty to gun possession charge, and getting the murders dismissed passed off a self-defense...the stand your ground law.

Jonas stood and nodded his head in approval, and said. "Nia this here is headquarters. Nobody knows about this place except you, Mark and myself.

"Aight." said Nia.

Jonas grabbed the duffle bag, and walked to the back of the cabin. Nia laid her head back on the couch and tried to relax her nerves.

Chapter 22

66 and Ashland Avenue was semi populated. People walked back and forth on both sides of the street, just enjoying the cool breeze. The temperature was still warm. But the sun was slightly going down by the minute.

A small crowd of people stood in line waiting to fill the Chicago Transit Authority (CTA) Bus. The crown was a mix of teenagers and the others were professionals getting off from a long day of work. They hurried getting on the bus. The CTA Bus pulled off slowly from the curb and slide its way into the dense traffic. A lonely person sat on the bench watching the Bus head North on Ashland Avenue.

Roscoe had just finished lining Diamond Dre's neck area. He snatched the black cap off Dre's body and gave him a mirror to look at his fresh shape-up.

"Yeah, this thing straight Ras."

"Like always." Roscoe said.

Dre stood up and reached into his pocket for some cash. He flipped through the knot of money, and handed Roscoe two twenties. The barber shop wasn't crowded on this particular day. A woman wearing a Dereon sun dress sat in the chair by the door. She had her legs crossed and a phone to her ear. The woman's son was in the chair across from her getting his hair cut by one of the barbers. Diamond walked to the huge mirror on the wall next to the woman. He gave his hair cut a second look, the woman disconnected the phone and stared and Diamond with a seductive look.

"What's up Diamond D?" She said.

"You already know it's about me."

She giggled at his conceded remark and uncrossed her legs.

Slow Motion had been parked across the street from Fresh Cutz barber shop for twenty minutes now. He grew frustrated at the job he was ordered to do, but Slow Motion knew he couldn't protest the request.

Diamond Dre sat down next to the seductive woman with the sexy sundress on. Her son frowned at the sight of Dre's hand rubbing the side of her legs. Cristine shot a glance at her son, but continued to let Dre rub on her. He whispered in Christine's ear and she shook her head, yes. Diamond pulled out his phone and dialed some number in it. "You locked in shorty." Dre told Christine. He got up from the seat and headed straight for the door.

"Roscoe, I'm see you next week Joe." Diamond said.

"Ay, make sure you call first. I got a couple things lined up, and I don't want to miss you when you come through." Roscoe said, as he swept the loose hair off the floor.

Roscoe had a nice low-key place. All the hustlers from Hustlers Row and throughout the Englewood came through to have their heads done by the best. And, Roscoe employed nothing but the best barbers out the GO. If you were on top of your cut game you had a booth in Fresh Cutz.

"Yo Diamond, it's still on for tonight right?" Malik asked.

Malik was one of Diamond's numerous customers he wasn't heavy in the game, but Malik spend enough money on a weekly bases to be able to cop weight directly from him.

"No doubt," Diamond said.

Slow Motion leaned forward to see if Diamond was actually going to leave this time out the shop. He had already alerted the Blondie wearing the dark sunglasses that was sitting alone on the bus stop.

"Daddy leaving now," Slow Motion said, and hung up the phone.

Diamond had his head down walking out the door reading a text message. Blondie on the bus stop speed walked, but had a slight limp, with it, up the sidewalk directly toward Diamond. He stopped for a minute looking at his phone again and then looked up at the person wearing a blond wig with dark shades. Fear immediately snatched his heart.

Blondie pulled a chrome .45 out of the small bag. Diamond froze looking down the barrel of the gun. BOOM! BOOM! Two head shots hit Dre, and he stumbled back into the door and fell on his face. Blondie stood over Dre, and fired two more shots. BOOM! BOOM!.

Slow Motion made a u-turn and within seconds was in front of the shop. People inside the barbershop scrambled to get out the line of fire. Diamond's body lay helpless on the sidewalk. Blondie jumped inside the Escalade Bobby Mackey snatched off the Blond wig.

"That's how GO niggas do shit!" Bobby Mackey shouted.

He was animated, as Slow Motion sped down Ashland.

"I don't know what's wrong with you young niggas, I'm back motherfuckers!" Bobby Mackey said.

Since the hit on Murders Row the GO had been super tense. B.O.G. had made a statement, and the body count was huge. Ten died, and had two was in critical condition. Blackout Gang was picking off so many Bogus Boyz. People wondered if any were left. But they took the hits, and continued to clap back at the B.O.G. in an attempt to show strength.

The ARIS had Bobby Mackey laid up for a few months, and word on the streets he left the GO for good and was living down in Florida. He had fooled them all except his boys. They knew he was straight. Bobby gave orders out dealing to them from his spot in the wild 100's. However, when you got a rep like Bobby Mackey you don't tuck your tail, and fold up shop. When you are outnumbered in war you have to do the unexpected, and that meant sitting back and thinking through your strategy.

"How you niggas let them bitch ass, B.O.G, niggas hit up Murders Row?" Bobby asked to no one in particular.

Slow Motion knew Bobby Mackey was on one, so he didn't respond.

"Ain't no nigga ever came to Murders Row, and did that shit, but get in line." Bobby screamed.

The police car got behind Slow Motion's Escalade.

"Damn the police are behind us." Slow Motion said.

Bobby Mackey looked through the passenger side mirror. The police was on their heels.

"Fuck" Bobby Mackey said.

Slow Motion tensed up behind the wheel and was in panic mode.

"Calm down my nigga we good." Bobby Mackey said. Bobby grabbed the 9mm from under the seat.

"Listen pull over on the next side street and if he turn with us stop by the alley and I'm going to light his ass up."

Slow Motion began to sweat a little bit because he knew Bobby Mackey was serious, and didn't want no part of a cops homicide. Slow Motion made a right turn on 62nd and Ashland, and the police hit his sirens and busted a U-turn toward 66 and Ashland.

"Scared ass nigga!" Bobby Mackey said, laughing.

"Nigga I ain't scared you tripping." Slow Motion said, smiling.

"We got that nigga, Diamond. That was for my little brother. Joey RIP my nigga; and the rest of the Bogus Boyz."

Bobby couldn't believe that Joey was murdered. He was still young, and didn't get a chance to live his life. The scene was devastating, and made the front page of Chicago's SCIN Times. Joey had been thrown into the street of 57th and Green. He was naked, and hog tied with 'B.O.G' carved into his chest. By the time, the cops had arrived to get him; he was stinking and had dried up blood caked all around his head and body.

Bobby was furious about the way Joey was thrown in the streets, and left like a dead animal carcass. He understood it though. The street had never showed any love, so why would they now. He knew what he had to do, though.

Even with his slight limp, he felt good. Bobby's mind was set on winning the war. The cast had came off and Bobby was back in action. Chicago's going to bleed. Its all he thought on the trip back to Murder's Row.

Chapter 23

J onas strolled through the Cancer Ward. As usually, he had a dozen red roses for his love. Doris loved them, and he knew this. So, he tried his best to make her feel a little better on each visit, even though he could see that the cancer was eating her alive. He still remained optimistic that she would pull through it, but he knew in the back of his head that wasn't possible. Doris had pancreatic cancer, and the cancer was destroying her liver at a rapid rate. The doctor's cutter, applied Chemo, and cut more trying to fight the disease, but their efforts were fruitless. They had been updating Jonas along the way. Doris didn't want to know. She directed, and fielded all questions about her condition to Jonas. Doris ordered the doctors to keep Jonas updated on her progress.

He moved past several patients and doctors. This part of the hospital was the saddest place. Death was evident in most of the patients. They were hopeless, scared and not wanting to embrace reality. That's what their demeanors displayed throughout the ward. Jonas hated the site, but he kept it to himself.

Jonas stood in front of her door, and knocked twice. He entered right after, Doris was sitting up in her wheelchair. She had and I pad lying in her lap, and surfed the internet. Yvonne had brought by the hospital a couple of days before. Right before Jonas dropped the bomb on her. He was through with her. Jonas had tried hard to keep her, but the constant nagging about his gang affiliation with the Blackout was too much for him. He had to much on his plate. Jonas held sole responsibility of people's lives, and wealth. Yvonne just couldn't understand it. She had thought that the fifty year sentence taught him a lesson. And, it did to a certain level. He would just never let her know this.

He walked over and kissed Doris on the forehead.

"Hey lady, I see you up, and moving about."

"Boy, I get so tired of that bed, I haven't slept so much since I was a teeny bopper." Doris smiled at the thought of her being young again.

A bright smile appeared across his face. Damn it was good to see my baby smile. Jonas thought to himself.

"How you feeling?"

"I'm holding it together."

Doris knew she needed a liver transplant, and that the chances of getting one was unconceivable especially, due to her being black, and from the Southside. She figured that they would give one to a more relevant person, who was probably undeserving of it.

"You look strong, Mom."

"I feel like I'm strong...Some days it's like this and other days it's tough."

"How you like the I pad?" He said, trying to switch the gloomy topic. Jonas grabbed a seat, and sat it next to her chair, then plopped down in it.

"Child, I have not put this thing down since Yvonne dropped it off."

He hadn't told Doris about him leaving Yvonne yet. She would be upset. Doris was big of loyalty and friendship. Yvonne had been a very supportive friend to her, during those days of Jonas's incarceration. When, Doris needed a shoulder to lean on, Yvonne was there. But, Doris would understand Jonas's reasons. Doris had come up in the streets. She knew that organized gang activity was a way of life in Chicago, so you had to deal with it. She had been very instrumental in Jonas's rise to power. As a mother and mentor, Doris had dated countless hustlers, and legends in the city. She knew what it took to achieve power, and keep it. Through the years, she soaked Jonas with all this knowledge. She figured it was better to teach him early on, before he fell victim to the streets, and became a low-life. That wouldn't amount to nothing in life. He took her advice, alone with some of the other legends like Larry Hoover, but Doris let him know what a solid structure was the key to everything. Family, business, and gang life, if you couldn't organize it and lead it, you were destined for failure.

Jonas just smiled at her happiness. "She told me you set up your FaceBook page."

"Yeah, and I got so many friends. Shit, I thought most of them were dead." She shook her head in disbelief of how many people actually were on the site.

"They showing me a lot of support on this damn thing."

"Yeah, they say everybody is on that joint." Doris looked over, and seen a lot of build up pressure in Jonas's face and demeanor. She knew the look well enough to know that something was on his mind. Doris read her kids like a book.

"I know you didn't come out here to talk about FaceBook, and this is not even one of your usual days... What's on your mind?"

"It's crazy out there, Mom."

"I know, I been seeing it all over the TV. and the internet. They say it's a war between the Bogus Boyz, and the Blackout Gang." Doris said, while shaking her head. "Jonas, that's not smart, baby. It's too early for all that killing to be going on while you're leading these people."

He knows better, but only if she knew that half of the problem was her daughter's fault. Because of her ordering Bobby's hit, none of this would've happened.

"Where's your sister? She hasn't been by lately."

"She's out in Vegas with Mark for a few days." He dropped his head, and lifted it back up.

"She has gotten out of control since I came home. I've never seen her act so crazy."

Doris shook her head. "Keep her safe for me. That's my baby there." She paused for a minute, while she reflected on Nia killing the two men who tried to rape her.

"Nia seen a lot in her life. All at a young age."

"I know! I'll never let anything happen to her."

"Good!" Doris said, trying to get out of the gloom past. "You know what you are going through is nothing new. Larry Hoover, Jeff Fort, Minister Rico, Bay-Bay, Angelo, Sam Lawrence and the rest of those gangsta's in Chicago have been through. You just got to take their lessons, or should I say failures, and do better."

Chicago always had a rich history of gangs. Going all the way back to the eighteen hundreds, and only a few have been able to maintain a level of respect, and influence. It was hard because Chicago didn't respect the weak or meek.

"I understand...I just don't think I'm up for this stuff anymore."

"What you going to do walk away?" Doris said.

Jonas knew that was impossible. Doris smiled at the thought.

"What?" asked Jonas.

"Son, you are a rare breed and to do what you've done with B.O.G is truly impressive. I mean only a few have done it."

"Mom, you don't understand."

She waved him off. Doris placed the I pad on her bed. "I know those streets of Chicago like the back of my hand. The game don't change, only the characters."

Jonas shook his head, and smiled at the feisty lady. It was clear where Nia got her attitude from.

"I know it gets ruff, but where you going? This is all we know." It was true. "your sister is going to challenge you at times until you put her ass in check. Remember this is a business. It's a lot of money at stake when you at the head of the table." Doris said

"We had a nice long talk, and I think she understands what's at stake."

"I told that girl when you come home to fall back, and enjoy life...She got enough damn money. Her and by baby Mark...She needs to go on and have me some grand kids before I leave this place."

"Mum, stop talking like that!"

Jonas didn't want to believe it, but he knew her time was limited. She had been waiting for awhile to get a liver transplant; and her name was near the end of the waiting list.

"I believe that power has become her drug of choice, and the streets are scared to death of her."

Doris chuckled at the thought. "She always wanted to be feared, and she got that now I see." She gave another light chuckle at Nia's craziness. "Paul, you need to arrange a meeting with all the gang leaders, and bring about some peace. All this killing is going to send you back to prison, and after all, nobody will be able to make any money in a little bit...It's enough now."

"I'm not sure it would work at this point."

"It'll work if you have a solid plan, and stand firm on a city wide truce." said Doris.

Jonas thought about the possibility a dozen times. He had got the blessings from Larry, and numerous other leaders about trying to bring some sort of peace amongst the groups. "Well, were only beefing with the Bogus Boyz, and they got a half insane leader, but I might be able to make this thing happen."

"Somebody within their group has got some type of influence, and he should be the one to go see."

Here he was thirty-five years old, and leading a gang of dope dealers and killers, but yet Doris was giving him much needed advice.

"First touch base with the other leaders, and secure a meeting. Start a board, and run it just like a Fortune 500 company. You can't loose." said Doris.

"I think it could work." Jonas saw the potential. Nobody had yet to try, and organize the city.

"Remember Jonas...Money is an illusion. That's going to be your weapon dangling the possibility of everybody gaining from the opportunity and living long enough to relish their riches."

"Mom, that's enough, I understand the goal."

He had to calm her down. Doris was trying to show Jonas a different angle that he could use his influence. She wanted him to reinvent himself, and bring calmness to the city.

Jonas kissed her on the cheek and helps her back in the bed. He tucked her in, and went over a few other things with her, then left. He had a new vision, a new outlook on the culture. With time, and patience, he envisioned that the leaders could actually organize themselves in a professional level. Gain political clout, and save a lot of lives in the process. He made his way towards the elevator. Angela turned the corner carrying a clip board. She was heading to Doris's room. Angela spotted him first. "Thanks for calling Paul." She said, and continued strolling past.

He looked over and smiled. The elevator door opened, and a few patients with family members exited.

"Excuse me come here for a second."

Angela immediately stopped; she stood there in the middle of the highway. Angela had on a colorfully designed top, smock with a pair of all white pants. Her all pink boy shorts like panties could be seen a tad bit when she walked. Jonas stopped a few inches from her.

"I'm sorry I didn't call. I been busy." He gave her a flirtatious smile, in a manly way "I tell you what, though. Dinner on me tonight at Queen of Sea."

He knew she was game for it. Any woman loved dinner at Queen of Sea. It was a nice exclusive spot that served great soul food.

"I don't know. You got a lot of gurus with you."

"I promised."

Angela wrote her address down, and gave it to him." You can pick me up at seven." She smiled. "Don't stand me up twice."

"I won't."

She strolled off, and put an extra twist in the switch. Jonas shook his head staring at the sexy woman. 'I got to get some of that' He thought, as she bent the corner glancing back at him.

Chapter 24

The sun was bright, and there had been silence through out the cemetery for almost a hour. The spacious cemetery was crowded. Limousines, cars, and SUV's crowded the parking lanes. Chauffeurs who were driving the limousines, waited patiently by their vehicles for the mourners to finish paying their respects to one of Chicago's finest hustler's.

Thirty Blackout members from Englewood were dressed in black suits made by Polo's, black label, brand. They wore dark shades, and ear pieces. Jonas was making a statement that the B.O.G was still strong and powerfully despite the deaths of comrades in the past months. These B.O.G members were on security. They sort of reminded you of Secret Service Agents, except these men were real life killers, and wasn't ashamed of it. They spread out, and inspected all vehicles that approached the burial area.

A large group of men, women, and children crowded around the burial site. A black casket sat above a deep hole, draped with white flowers around it. The mood was somber, and sad.

Diamond Dre was beloved throughout Chicago. Everyone interacted with Dre because he was fair, and never quick to judge a person based off a flaw they might have had. He made sure every person around him made money, and those that he dealt with on a regular. Chicago took his lost hard, and turn out at his burial was clear. Some had attended the actual funeral, but others participated in following Dre's last ride. Jonas had ordered that Diamond be driven through Englewood one last time before being taken to his resting place. Englewood represented to the fullest. They were lined on both sides of the street with RIP signs, t-shirts, B.O.G for life and waving their last good-byes to Diamond, as he passed by in the limo.

Jonas and Nia were posted up in the front surrounded by a small team of soldiers, all from Hustler's Row. Jonas maintained throughout the show of support, but Diamond Dre's murder bothered him the most. More than Bolo's murder, Jonas had taken Dre under his wing, as a little brother. Even though, Dre was only two years younger than him at the age of thirty-three.

After Dre's murder Jonas had proposed the idea of forming a Board for all the major street gangs throughout Chicago. To his surprise, everyone jumped on the idea immediately except the Bogus Boyz of course. Jonas had tried again to reach out and end the beef. A representative tried to convince Bobby to get on board only to be returned in a body bag.

The gangs got together within days of the announcement at an undisclosed location on the outskirts of Chicago. They put the board together, and voted for Jonas to be the chairman. Jonas now had slowly maneuvered his way to achieving a goal that at first seemed impossible in the hectic politics of Chicago gang activity.

Dre's funeral was proof of the Board's sincerity of coming together on a common goal: stopping the killing and getting back to making money. All the street gangs were in attendance. This was one of the board's first tests of solidarity, and they passed with flying colors. These same groups had killed each other's best friends, family members and kids, but yet they wanted to put it all behind them now.

Jonas had made Diamond; co-chairman in death, though, the position was simply symbolic in nature.

Nia grabbed Jonas's hand, as the preacher begun to speak. Just like Jonas, she hated funerals. A lot of people would've been surprised at the revelation. Being as though, she placed a lot of men there.

"From God we come and to God we return. May God have mercy on De'andre Johnson's soul." The Preacher said, and then made a religious gesture in the form of a cross. The casket was slowly lowered into the ground. A few people tossed flowers into the grave, as the casket continued to be lowered.

Jonas walked toward the parking lot, and the large crowd parted ways to make a lane for him, ad the mourning family. His soldiers were on high alert. As Jonas moved through the crowd, leaders of the numerous gangs simply nodded. They were giving him their silent condolences.

Nia and Trina followed a few steps behind him.

"Girl, I think I'm pregnant." Nia whispered to Trina. She was tired of holding the secret in. Trina nodded her head with a delighted smile.

"You'll make a good mother." Trina said, and then hugged her slightly while walking. "Does Mark know?"

"Nah, I haven't told him yet."

"You need to tell him A.S.A.P."

Nia always respected Trina like a big sister, because she always spoke her mind, and never cared what people thought about it. Maybe because she was a killer. They both were alike, but yet different in many ways.

"Damn, Mark is going to be pumped." Nia said to herself.

Mark had been waiting for years to have kids. Nia wanted them too, but always made sure she was on the pill. At the time, she was too entranced in the streets. Nia didn't need the extra liability that having a kid came with. Now, that mark was settled, and their future looked a little secure in Las Vegas, it was the perfect time for the couple.

Jonas got escorted to his bullet proof Cadillac limousine. He was followed by Nia, Trina and Flip Toney. They got in the vehicle, and settled down in the back.

"Damn, when were you going to tell me?"

"What?" Nia asked surprised.

"About the baby," said Jonas.

Nia just waved her hand in a playful manner at Jonas. He smiled, and leaned over to hug her. "Congratulations, baby sis!"

"Thank you." Nia said, smoldered in his hug.

Everyone in the limo began to clap and congratulate Nia. She was happy, and excited from their reaction. A light tear rolled down her face. She tried to hurry up and wipe it, but it was too late. The tears just started flowing.

Chapter 25

Three Months Later

T he sky was clear, and the sun beamed down on the customers seated outside the coffee shop. They sat around drinking their coffee, talking, and enjoying the mid-seventies temperature on an October afternoon.

A black Envoy pulled into the small parking lot followed by a tan Toyota Camry. Roger Freeman exited the dark tinted Envoy. He was dressed regular in jeans, and a long sleeve plaid shirt. Roger waited for a second to hit the alarm on his SUV and then Angela stepped out of her Camry. She was off of work today, from her hospital job, and needed to talk. But, not just to anyone. Angela had been going through an emotional roller coaster lately, since she started dating Jonas. She came to the conclusion that she needed to exit the case quickly. Angela had started getting to relaxed, and attached to her suspect, and she hated herself for it. She had sworn to herself before that she would never go undercover again. The secrets that came with it, the emotional experience that followed, and unexpected behaviors that came from the suspects, and she was just too much to handle.

Angela strolled towards Roger. She threw her tan pocket book strap over her white short sleeve shirt, and then fixed her expensive denim jeans. They both walked into Starbucks without saying a word to each other. This was routine behavior, while undercover. Roger played it cool, as if he didn't know her at first, until he scanned the store to see if any potential people was in the store that could recognize him. They had decided on meeting in Skokie, IL. the night before. The place was north of Chicago, and took forty-five minutes to get there from Chicago's city limits. It was a quiet town, with no signs of gangsters or gang violence. The place was perfect for them.

Roger headed to the back of Starbucks, and sat at a table with a window view of the parking lot. Angela had stopped at the counter, and ordered a double latte. Then headed towards the back, and took a seat across from Roger.

He didn't waste no time. "What's so urgent?" He asked in a concerned voice.

"I'm backing out this case...I'm not sure I have what it takes to move forwards." She was confused.

"What does that supposed to mean?"

Angela took a sip of her coffee. She tried to remain calm, and professional. She didn't want to reveal the obvious to Roger. Angela was in love, but tried to convince herself it was lust. Over the last couple of months the two became an item. Angela tried hard to fight off the emotions, but she couldn't. Jonas showed her to much attention that nobody else since, Anthony showed her, and a great time along with it. They went on movie dates, dinner dates, and even caught a playoff game together. Angela tried her best to drill it in her head that he was a suspect. A killer, drug dealer, gang banger, and just plain filth she tried to think of him as nothing but his actions showed different. Jonas made it hard for her to think of him in those types of ways, and she hated him for that. At least, she wanted to hate him, but she couldn't.

"I just think I'm in too deep, and would like to change course."

"Listen, we're inside the B.O.G. for the first time, and we need to build this case, and get them bastards off the streets."

Angela just gazed at Roger. You're the bastard asshole. She thought to herself, while Roger tried to convince her to stay on the case.

"Have you been to his condo in the Water Tower?" asked Roger.

She nodded her head, and thought about their first night there. "Yes, I've been there."

"Good. Now, we can go apply for a few bugs to place around the condo."

"Have you heard anything I just told you?" Angela said annoyed at his question. She wanted out there would be no bugs placed, no statements of their activities documented, and no warrants for phone taps applied for.

Roger leaned over the table "Listen, you're given a direct order to stay on this case. Washington gave me you and you're going to help build this case for the agency." He said in a quiet forceful manner.

Angela stared at Roger with scorn written all over her face. He was placing her in an uncomfortable situation. She thought about her career first, then her daughter and mother. What would they think of her? Angela needed to do what was best for her. "Okay mutha fucka! I told you from the beginning I couldn't deal with this shit, but I'm going to do my job." She gathered her things, and stood up to leave. Roger grabbed her by the arm.

"Remember, you made an oath to protect and serve." He said, then let loose of Angela's arm. She stormed off out of the store.

Nakira sat on the teal sofa. She had on a pair of tiny boy shorts and a matching tank top with no socks on. Nakira strolled through her Blackberry for any news worthy information. She was an information junkie. She loved staying in tuned to what was going on around the state, country, and world. It was a habit she picked up while attending the police academy.

Jonas walked out of the hallway wearing a pair of jeans, and a wife-beater. The two had spend the weekend together in Nakira's sister house, Keisha, who lived on the Southside of Chicago. He stepped over her legs stretched across the wooden table, and took a seat beside her.

The two had basically known each other their whole lives. They grew up a few houses from each other on 66th and Justine, and had an on and off relationship since their childhood years except of course when he was not in juvi hall, or the county jail, which was rare at the time. Their relationship lasted for years until they were adult's. With his constant prison stays, and her ambitions to do better in life, Jonas felt it was better to separate, and just remain friends. She agreed. He encouraged Nakira to follow her dreams, and become the police officer she had dreamed to be. Everybody else thought she was crazy for having the idea except Jonas. She took his advice, and headed to the academy, and Jonas was sent to prison for murder.

Nakira got the job, and worked hard behind the scene to help Jonas. She secretly got her hands on documents and information that the prosecutor had withheld from Jonas's lawyers. The task was hard and it took years, but by her being in the law enforcement field, and men constantly trying to impress her with their positions of authority, she made it happen. Jonas asked how she gained access to the State Attorney's records, but she wouldn't reveal her strategy. It was a secret she was taking to the grave. Nakira wouldn't tell anyone.

Jonas rubbed her smooth toned leg, and then stopped to put his shirt on. Nakira just gave him a worried stare. She was still in love with her first love after all of these years, but she knew it was impossible for her to be in his life. Especially at this moment of time. She placed the Blackberry on her lap, and looked at him fixing his navy blue Polo shirt.

"Ken-Ken agreed to cooperate, and wear a wire on you." Nakira said, while reaching under the sofa to retrieve a folder.

"What! When did he get locked up?" Jonas thought he still was hiding out, and running from the authorities. Damn! He thought.

After, Ken-Ken got arrested he agreed to cooperate, but got scared, and skimped town. He remained in contact with the Night Stalker, but he had second thoughts of cooperating. Once out, he made a call to Jonas, and explained to him about how he had to get out of town because the police had found the drugs in his truck, and they had an arrest warrant out for him. Jonas agreed it was best that he stayed out of town, and fell back until everything blew over. Jonas just didn't know that he had agreed to help the cops. Nakira knew though, and waited for the opportune time to tell Jonas.

"This is his entire statement." She handed Jonas the folder. He took a couple minutes going through it. he placed the folder back on the table, and started pacing the floor.

"So, has he got me on any phone conversations, yet?"

"No. He didn't get a chance, but he's coming back to Chicago this week, and he's going to want to meet you."

Jonas just stared at her. He was furious at her. Why wait, so long to tell him. She must've had her reasons. He thought.

"I appreciate this, and all the other favors you been doing for me."

"Word around the force is that the DEA got somebody inside ya circle, so be careful of who you let close to you."

"DEA?" Jonas was surprised at the information. Maybe it was somebody from the board? He tried to rack his brain for any new faces. Jonas couldn't though. His mind was to pre-occupied with Ken-Ken's betrayal.

"That's what we've been briefed on by the Chief." Nakira said, with a serious tone.

"Thanks! You always there for me when it counts."

He walked over to her. Nakira stood up from the sofa. Her athletic body, and beautiful features confused a lot of people she was thirty-five, but looked like she was still twenty-five. Jonas grabbed her by the waist, and gave her a long and passionate kiss.

"I got to go sweetheart."

"Be safe...Jonas." She dropped her head and then looked back up to him in the eyes. "I love you, and don't ever forget that."

"I know." He said, and gave her a playful smack on her rare end.

Jonas stepped outside the home, and headed for his Ford F-350 parked across the street. He was out, and about in the city, so he tried to remain low-key by driving the truck. Bobby was still roaming around, so he didn't want to take no chances of being noticed.

A black Envoy sat at the top of 66th and Woods the agent on the passenger side took pictures rapidly of Jonas exiting the home, and getting into the truck.

"I think we got enough pictures."

"Yeah, put it up now before somebody looks out the window, and see you."

Jonas pulled off quickly from the curb. The Envoy wanted for awhile and then followed Jonas.

Chapter 26

The Silver Range Rover drove smoothly up the quiet street. Trina sat behind the wheel with a determined look. She scanned the area, while keeping the wheel steady. It was more, or so her instincts if nothing else. The quiet community in Naperville, on the outskirts of Chicago, was by far too exclusive and extremely wealthy for any of Chicago's gangs to have any altercations inside of the vicinity. Trina's real worries were being tailed to the home. Her concern was nothing, but the police this day.

Ken-Ken had the crew on high alert. After Jonas got the word of his betrayal he immediately called a meeting with the board. It was a must. He could've kept to himself, and just get rid of the problem, but Jonas had morals, dignity, and loyalty to the board and B.O.G. Ken-Ken got knocked off before the alliance, but Jonas felt a duty to let the board know what was up

As Trina was slowly passing a handcrafted custom detailed home with a black suburban in the driveway, she looked in on the white man leaning up against the truck talking with a woman. The man glanced at the tinted up Range passing by. The pale looking extremely, thin, white woman didn't even grace at the truck.

"You think that's a decoy?"

Jonas glanced at the couple from the passenger side. "Nah, you don't have anything to worry about." He gave Trina a sincere grin. Jonas was confident that no undercover, agents or any other form of law enforcement was tailing them. Nakira had laid out the plan for him. The Chicago PD was strictly going to use Ken-Ken, as their weapon. They figured an inside source this time would put Jonas behind bars for life. He could provide them with countless incriminating conversations, murders that took place, and all the numerous ways B.O.G distributed its drugs to the streets of Chicago. The plan was a slam dunk at least they thought.

"Them crackers ain't no cops!" yelled Nia from the backseat. She turned and kept her eye on the couple as the Range continued up the street.

"Like I told the two of you before, nobody knows about his cooperation yet. My people told me that this was their best option. So, we don't have to worry about none of that bullshit."

"I'm still staying on point baby boy."

"What we need to be worried about is if any of the neighbors seen any of the homies pulling up to the house."

"Jonas, we good on that."

"Nia, you with me how you know?"

"I got a text from Flip earlier."

Trina pulled into the concrete driveway. A stunning stucco and stone home accented the estate. A Grand Cherokee and a Black Denali sat parked in a row in front of the two car garage. She drove up to the left side of the garage, and stopped. Nia reached over her shoulder with a black garage remote, and aimed it at the door. She hit the little red button. The left side of the garage lifted up smoothly. Trina pulled up and parked the Range. Jonas was the first to get out, followed by Nia getting out and hitting the switch again. The garage door came back down, and quietly closed. Jonas moved through the spacious garage with ease. An all black BMW 750 was parked on the right side.

Jonas glided his hand over the hood. "I see Flip been waiting a long time for us."

Other than the two cars, the garage was completely empty. Crème tilts on the walls, and a concrete floor with two small windows on each door of the garage brought life to the space

The luxury home was the Board's secret meeting spot. Major decisions about Chicago's underworld were made in this tucked away place. Through his connections, Mark had found the place for Nia, It was the first of many safe houses the group would all chip in to rent. The place was being leased under Mark's company name to avoid any traces coming back to any of the leaders. It was a win-win situation for all. The bills would be paid out of the treasury funds, which all of the board contributed too, and it was off limits to anybody that was not a board member.

Nia strolled over to the wooden door. She grabbed the handle and then stopped all of a sudden, "Shit!" She looked over to the small box posted up on the wall. Nia lifted the glass cover and hit a few numbers into the system. She turned, and stared at Jonas walking up behind Trina. "I almost forgot the alarm code"

"Yeah, I know" Jonas said, smiling.

Nia went and opened the door. Trina followed her through the hallway. Jonas closed the door behind him and followed the woman through the home. They arrived in the kitchen. Three white leather stools with black trimming and chrome frames sat at the glass table with wooden sides and white edges. A stainless steel refrigerator occupied the back of the kitchen; white wooden cabinets with glass doors surrounded the room. The kitchen was huge and the Granite Island screamed wealth.

The house was top notch with a highly advanced alarm system. Even though nobody lived in the home the board still wanted it secure from any attempts by law enforcement to break in and plant wires and bugs.

The cherry wood floors gleamed, as the three strolled through the place. A long wooden table occupied the living room placed squarely in the middle. All the heads of Chicago's notorious underworld sat around the table. Some smoked cigarettes others talked amongst each other, while drinking sodas and water. Flip sat at the corner of the table with a phone to his ear. He eyed Jonas coming through the doors, and immediately hung up the phone. Flip knew he had just violated a rule of the house. Jonas had made it clear to everyone that no phones were to be used when they were at the meetings. It was strictly for security purposes. For the simple reasons that the phones, while in use could be traced to the time, area, and space of where you were at using information from the cellular tower. And that wasn't good for business. The group wanted to be in the dark with their activities.

Jonas headed in the room, and missed Flip's quick, but discrete concealment of the phone. He smiled and kept a confident walk at the thought of his achievements. Jonas had brought ten of Chicago's most respected gang leaders together under a treaty. These ten men including Jonas accounted for almost hundred thousand members under their control. At the drop of a dime, if organized right, and well planned out they could take control of the city of Chicago. The gangs were well armed and had tremendous heart. Jonas had his doubts, especially the other leaders that were incarcerated now and denoted by the prison system. Only his mentor Larry Hoover, Old Man as he called him believed in Jonas's vision. So with the Old Man blessings and his goal to do the unthinkable in the city, Jonas planned daily. He mingled in the joint with the other gang members while still repping B.O.G. On the streets Jonas had Nia spreading the word that B.O.G. had the work for cheap, and then upon his release Jonas combined all his recourses and made his move.

P-Town, leader of the Gangsta Disciples stood-up out his seat, and strolled over to greet Jonas with a handshake. "What's up? I came as soon as you called." P-Town was concerned about the emergency meeting. The GD's were B.O.G. biggest alliance before the creation of the board. Jonas had mad respect for how the GD's flipped a street gang into a political movement with a purpose, while still keeping their street credit.

"I'm glad you had time to stop by. I'm going to break the news to the whole board."

P-Town took a seat, and slouched back in the chair. Nia and Trina waved and said their hello's to everybody, then took a seat at the table. After Dre was murdered Jonas made Trina a trusted member of B.O.G.

Jonas was the only one, who remained standing. "I'm glad y'all made it out here on such a short notice, but I felt as though this information I received should be shared with the board immediately." He looked around the room. Everyone paid close attention. "As I said before we are only as strong as our weakest link, and our demise, if it should come will start internally. We have a snitch in the midst of us."

Pablo from the Latin Kings looked around the table trying to sense any weakness in the group. The others did the same. The room grew tense, and everybody was ready to go back to the pre-treaty days.

"No need to be alarmed...I already know who the culprit is. He was amongst the trusted members of B.O.G."

Flip face grimaced from the remark. He hated rats with a passion. Flip's brother, and father had been betrayed by their, so called friends, and both received life sentence in the Feds.

"Who is it?" Pookey from the Vice Lords asked in a harsh tone.

Jonas just stared at him. "Ken-Ken" He shook his head in disgusted. "He had been arrested not to long ago and they flipped him. So he agreed to help them build a case and take me down. The theory is with me out the way B.O.G would crumble...They plan, and we plan, and I think we have the upper hand. The fact of the matter is clear that with every strong movement there are rats amongst the group...Our study is to limit the damage."

Chicago PD was only interested in the activities of Blackout Gang from day one since Jonas left the joint. The shooting of Bobby and the murders that followed increased the pressure to bring down B.O.G. The cops had no idea about the new alliances that was made. Ken-Ken didn't know about the treaty either.

They wanted him to trap Jonas up either on tape with drugs, selling drugs, buying drugs and to get him on tape discussing past and present murders. Chicago PD had pushed to get Jonas off the streets ten years ago, and in the process the prosecutor used false testimony, withheld evidence from the defense and paid witness to lie. The case was overturned and he walked free. B.O.G having a heavy presence in Chicago made Jonas a target.

"Now since someone from my click ratted, it's B.O.G job to take care of the problem...and we will do so."

Everybody shook their heads in agreement except Shabazz from the Blackstone's. He sat there and contemplated speaking his mind. Shit I run my own territory; Shabazz thought to himself and spoke. "What if we see him before any of your people's get him? Are we to just let a rat roam and build cases on good men throughout the GO? You know Ken-Ken was that dude in the city with the work and fucked with a lot of good men."

Sleepy D from the Manic Latin folks shook his head in agreement with Shabazz.

"As we speak I got a team tracking him down. Believe me none of you will have to worry about this problem I'm going to handle the situation."

"You still didn't answer my questions!"

Jonas struggled to hold his composure. "Shabazz y'all voted me chairman of the board, so please accept my judgment. And I ask that nobody take revenge out on him. B.O.G will handle this problem."

Shabazz just shook his head in disgust at Jonas's reply. He didn't like it one bit, and it showed on his face. It wasn't just B.O.G's problem; it was the board's problem Sleepy D thought to himself.

"Now since Ken-Ken pushed that work all over the city I think its best we get word out and have the men change up their connections. I still got a direct line to the main man and have chosen a small team to fill the void. They will layout a new plan of how we move the work in the coming days. Right now I think we should cut the flow of the work into Chicago and create a drought of sorts. With the drought we can up the prices and take more control of the city."

Jonas scanned the room and everyone was nodding their heads in agreement.

"I like the idea of the drought." Shabazz said.

"Listen the ten of us run the GO and these niggas out here will move as we say move...Also, we have told other niggas in the GO who are pushing big work that if they don't fuck with us we will shut their spots down."

Jonas had put together a small group and hollered at all the major dudes in Chicago, who were not a part of the board alliance to either cope with them or shut down shop. Jonas sat down and scanned the room. Nia stood up.

"As you all know I use to run the B.O.G. when Jonas was in the joint, and I answered to no one but him. So it's kinda hard for me to stand here, and do what I'm doing. But, I'm doing it to be a team player. We were beating around the bush about this clown Bobby Mackey for too long. The city is in an uproar because of this clown. I think now is the time we come together and vote on his demise .... What I'm asking for is a green light on his bitch ass."

The board all looked at each other trying to gauge everyone else reaction. Boosie from the Black Disciples was the only one in the group with a biased opinion. Omar was his main man. The two came up together in the Calumet building, tricked junkies together as youngsters, and even went to war with some GD's back in the day. He wasn't really close to Bobby, but he knew Bobby ran Murders Row for Omar. Boosie didn't want to cross Omar. But he knew Bobby had to go. He tried to tell Omar to sit Bobby down, but it didn't happen. Bobby was bad for business, and the success of the board was priority number one.

One at a time everyone gave their silent approval with the nod of the head. "Good! Now let all the soldiers know that Bobby and the Bogus Boyz got a green light on them."

It was already understood by Omar and the soldiers from the Bogus Boyz that Bobby was a liability. He was stopping the flow of money. Murders Row became a hot spot for the police after all the murders, and Chicago PD set up shop 24/7 on the Row. And if they ever wanted a voice in the city that Bobby had to go. But all of them didn't feel that way. Bobby still had a couple loyal soldiers going to ride with him.

"Well, fellas that's all for the day. I'll see everyone in a few weeks for our monthly meeting if nothing else comes up."

Everyone rose from their seats and headed toward the kitchen. Jonas grabbed Nia by the arm and whispered into her ear

"I like how you dealt with that." Nia smiled.

"I learned from the best."

Chapter 27

S hay's chrome Acura XR raced down Cottage Grove. The traffic was heavy for a Friday. Everyone was trying their best to get home and relax, and kick back for the weekend. Shay was in a hurry to see her baby. It had been a few months now, since she got the word of Ken-Ken's arrest. At first she was scared. Her soul mate and everything had finally been caught. Shay had dreaded the day of his eventual arrest. It was just a matter of time. Ken-Ken had been hustling since his youth and Shay had always been by his side. He had been arrested before throughout their relationship. Guns, minor possession charges and a couple assaults got dismissed. When Jonas plugged Ken-Ken with the connection, he became that dude in the GO. He had work when no one else had work. He was considered a solid dude, but never had Ken-Ken been caught with suck a huge amount red-handed. Shay just knew it had to be a mistake though. He would never ride around with all those drugs, and guns. She had thought. Until he gave her the real rundown of what happened on that fateful day.

She stopped at the red light on 71st and Cottage Grove. The large white framed Gucci sunglasses covered her pecan complexion. Shay stared in the rear view mirror to make sure nobody was following her. She had been nervous lately. Ken-Ken explained to her how important it was that she remains calm, and normal. He didn't want her to alter any of her routines, or alert anyone of his arrest. Shay had found it strange that he didn't want anybody knowing about the incident. She didn't pay it any mind though. He was home now, and she needed to see him bad. The light turned green. Shay hit the pedal hard. The Acura darted out in front of the whole crowd of cars, trucks, and buses.

Trina walked over to her Range Rover. The black Vera Wang cat suite hugged her tight body. She paused for a second, and kneeled down. Her freshly painted white tipped toe nails were snuggled together in a pair of open toe orange Louis Vuitton shoes. Trina rubbed her pinky toe and then stood up. For the past couple of days her toe had been giving her problems. She had injured it rushing out of the bed. After Nia called saying they knew where Ken-Ken hideout was at.

Trina glanced both ways, and climbed into the Range. Nia lounged on the passenger side with her legs crossed. She had on a pair of white red bottom Loubitons, and denim jeans with a tight all white Gucci t-shirt. Nia held a walkie-talkie in her hand. The Glock 9mm lay between her legs.

"You need to take that tight ass shirt off girl...Ya stomach need room to grow."

"Bitch please...I'm only a couple months pregnant. I'm not even showing yet."

"Yeah, because you stay wearing some tight ass shirts...I'm going to kick ya ass if my god baby come out fucked up."

"Girl, my baby is not going to come out fucked up." They giggled together.

Trina pulled off, and into traffic. Nia turned the radio up and J.Hudson "I got this" blasted through the speakers. Trina followed the 2013 burgundy Cadillac OTS.

Two soldiers from B.O.G. were inside the Cady. Meeko, a short dark skin youngster from Hustler's Row pushed the vehicle. He was an up and coming member. Rock sat back on the passenger side. His Chicago White SOX fitted was pulled low over his head. The only thing you could see was his smooth brown skin, and baby face. They both were dressed in black Dickie sets. Trina had handpicked the two nineteen year olds. She had watched them grow up on Hustler's Row, and seen some potential in them. Let alone she had a thing for Rock. He was a cutie she thought. Trina had plans for him, if he proved his loyalty to B.O.G. Now that she was running the distribution aspect of the board, she had clearance to dump the work on whomever, and Rock was on her list. Trina planned to make him important in the B.O.G structure, get some money, and if he followed her orders correctly, her little sex sweetie on the side.

"We heading up to the Twenty Grand Hotel. Y'all know how crowded it is up there, so don't make a move until I say so!"

Nia had second thoughts of hitting Ken-Ken in the middle of town. Twenty Grand hotel sat in the heart of the city, although it could be done. There were too many witnesses. She mixed the ideas it wouldn't be the first time somebody got killed in the middle of the business district of Chicago The car was stolen. Nia thought to herself. She went back and forth with herself the whole ride over whether she should do it. Jonas didn't like too much heat, and knocking Ken-Ken block off in the middle of town would sure bring out the media. The GO was on fire with all the murders, and the Chicago PD and Feds were starting to hit the city hard.

Nakira had given Jonas the full layout of Ken-Ken's cooperation. Along with the hotel he was staying at. They kept his arrest quiet, and out of the news-paper so he was free to roam the streets. He had already lied to Jonas that he skipped town after being let out.

Ken-Ken snatched a cloth off the hotel's rack. He turned on the hot water placed the rag under semi hot water took it out and squeezed it dry. Ken-Ken looked in the circle mirror at himself while wiping his face off. He was stressed and you could see it all in his face. Weed, liquor, pills and worry took a toll on him the past months or so.

"Fuck it, it's either them or me and I'm surely not coming out the loser in this one. I'm do this shit and take my ass down south to Alabama." Ken-Ken said, softly to himself.

He finished wiping his face and placed the wash cloth neatly back on the towel rack, and walked out the bathroom. A large queen size bed with the covers all messy sat against the wall. Two desks with lamps sat on each side of the bed. He went to the built in wall safe and opened the door. Two Glock 9mm lay in the safe with stacks of money. Ken-Ken grabbed a stack of money, and one 9mm. He stared at the gun, and put it back in the safe. The flat screen TV on the wall had IDb and Park on with videos playing and Roci looking good. "Damn I like shorty." Ken-Ken mumbled, as he watched Roci do her thing. A three foot nightstand was under the flat screen. Small gadgets, wires, and a tape recorder laid across the stand. Today was his day off to do as he pleased, and tomorrow he was to begin building a case against Jonas for the Chicago PD. "I got to hit Evergreen Plaza, and get me some gear" Ken-Ken mumbled.

Ken-Ken stopped at the table and start messing with the material. He pulled his shirt off revealing his slim frame with no chest hair. The years of weed smoke, pills, liquor and sex had slimed him down. The more money he got the more he ripped and ran the streets. He put his Polo t-shirt back on.

Ken-Ken had decided today was the day he would come out of hiding. He had to make it right with Jonas first though. His phone was blowing up a few days ago he wanted to call Jonas to gauge his reaction but knew Jonas wouldn't want an explanation over the phone. Ken-Ken knew that would be a stupid move to do. If he did that Jonas would clearly think something was up with him. They never talked about business over the phone. He paced the room in deep thought. "Fuck Jonas."

Shay smiled and sang Mary J's "Mr. Wrong" with the radio. At the end of the song she turned the radio down, and reached up to fix the mirror. Shay's diamond tennis bracelet fell down her arm; she shook her head in disbelief. 'No she can't be following me'

The red Caravan had been following her from the time she left the Englewood neighborhood. It was a woman behind the wheel though. So Shay thought nothing of it.

Shay pulled up to the curb, and double parked in the streets boxing herself in. Her hazard lights were on.

Streams of people were coming out of the entrance door of the hotel. Ken-Ken seen Shay's car pull up, and he headed out the lobby all smiles.

Trina was parked further down on the other side of the street. From their view they could see the entrance of the hotel.

The burgundy Cady had been circling the block every minute because Nia had still been undecided.

Ken-Ken came into Nia's view. She snatched the walkie talkie off her lap. "Listen hit Ken-Ken only do not hit Shay, GO! GO!" she yelled. Nia had known Shay since high school, and knew she didn't have anything to do with Ken-Ken being a snitch.

Trina let a few cars past, and pulled out into traffic. Nia clutched the Glock. Ken-Ken made it to the Acura. Shay reached over, and hugged and kissed him.

Rock clutched the AR15, as the Cady got held up behind a car. The red Caravan pulled along side of Shay's vehicle. The side door slide open. A masked man jumped out, he trotted with a limp. Shay was so much into the kiss that she didn't even pay attention to the area. Ken-Ken saw a masked man leap on the hood. His eyes darn near popped out his head. Ken-Ken pulled away from Shay, and cradled her body with his.

The masked man was standing on top of the hood, and let the Choppa loose on both of them. BAK! BAK! BAK! BAK! BAK! The bullets ripped through his body. Shay was getting hit from the bullets coming through Ken-Ken's body. Both of them was dead before the bullets stop flying.

"What the fuck? Follow that shit! Follow that fucking van!" Nia yelled through the walkie. She was pissed somebody else hit Ken-Ken. This was B.O.G's business. She thought, whoever hit him would pay for sure.

Trina got into straight gangster mode.

"Nah bitch, we on ya ass today," Trina said.

The masked man jumped off the Acura, and dove into the caravan. Cindy, a young chick, pulled off when she seen him fully inside the vehicle.

Trina tried to pull a long side of the caravan, but was stopped by a few cars stuck in traffic. They had been traumatized by the shooting. A large crowd quickly formed after the shooting stopped. Trina still remained boxed in, and couldn't get out with the caravan.

"Tell Rock to dump on them now, they about to get away." Trina screamed.

The caddy was stuck three cars back, and couldn't move.

"Hit'em now! NOW!" Trina yelled at Nia.

Cindy maneuvered out of traffic she floored the Caravan, and just like that she was gone.

The masked man kneeled down on the floor. The backseats of the Van had been pulled out, so he had enough room to move around. "Cindy, hurry up and get out of here." She hit the pedal hard, and made a right turn doing 60 mph darn near flipping the van over. "Oh shit!" she mumbled.

Cindy made it to safety. They ditched the van on a side street, and got into a black on black Escalade.

Nia was furious they missed the hit.

"Who the fuck was that?"

"I don't know, but I'm mad as hell that we got caught up between them cars."

Trina was still checking for the van. Although, she knew it was long gone. They floated around checking all the alleyways and side streets to see if or where they ditched the van. The Cadillac followed them on their pursuit.

Police sirens could be heard all around the area. Nia held the walkie to her mouth. "Ay, we going to meet y'all at the spot. Ditch the car too." She didn't wait on a response. Nia dropped the walkie in her lap, and grabbed her cell and punched in a number.

"Jonas, we got a problem."

"What's good?"

"They went against our word."

"Who?"

"Somebody just killed Ken-Ken and Shay outside the twenty grand."

"Shit."

"I think -." Jonas cut Nia off.

"Meet me over at the hospital I'm on my way to see mom dukes."

"Aight." Nia ended the phone call, and threw the phone on the dashboard.

"I been playing nice for the last few months, fuck that shit now...I'm going to bring the heat to all them niggas... I bet you Shabazz had something to do with this."

The old Nia was emerging at this point. Quite as kept, Nia never liked the idea of the Board she felt B.O.G. ran the city and everyone else fell in line. Through all her years of hugging the block, respect was a must, and now they hit Ken-Ken. That was a clear sign on disrespect.

"I told Jonas not to fuck with them niggas."

"Nia, calm down, remember you got a baby inside you."

Nia just stared out the window. "Take me to Holy Cross Hospital."

Chapter 28

J onas walked through the door, and Doris was lying motionless in the bed. She didn't move when the door opened. Jonas kissed her on the forehead. "Mom, how you feeling?" Doris didn't respond. Every time she had chemo treatment it took all her energy.

Jonas pulled up a chair, and held her hand. Damn mom you got to beat this shit baby girl. He thought without saying.

"Get me some water." Doris asked in a low voice.

Jonas sprang out the chair and grabbed the water picture with the straw and gave it to her.

"How are you son?"

"I'm good baby girl."

Nia entered the room and Doris smiled at the sight of her daughter. She hadn't seen her in weeks.

"Get your ass out that bed!" Nia said, laughing.

Doris smiled.

Nia kissed her on the lips. "I love you Mom."

Nia grabbed Doris hand and rubbed her belly with Doris hand. "We got another Jonas on the way."

"Come here."

Nia leaned down. "What's up?"

"You take care of yourself"

Doris was proud of Nia because she knew how tough Chicago was, and for Nia to survive amongst sharks was big.

Thank you lord, please protect my baby were Doris thoughts.

Jonas loved to see Doris, and Nia interact with each other. They had more of a sister relationship than mother daughter. Doris couldn't stop smiling as Nia talked.

"Mom, Mark and I are going to move you out to Vegas... The weather is better for your recovery."

"Child, I ain't going to nobody Las Vegas."

"Jonas tell her she is going."

"Child, Jonas ain't my daddy."

They all laughed

Jonas wanted her to go, but he knew she would never leave Chicago. She loved the city to much. Her wishes were to die there also.

"How they treating you out here? You know I'll tear this motherfucker up about you."

"You just worry about that baby in your stomach I'm okay."

"I'm glad you came out here Nia because she was barely talking."

"She know when I come out here its on, and she better talk." Nia said, smiling.

"Girl, you a damn fool just like your daddy."

Nia blushed hard. She liked to be told she was like her daddy, a real legend in Chicago.

"Have you checked your email? I sent you plenty of pictures from Vegas."

"Nah, not yet."

Nia grabbed the ipad, and handed it to Doris. "Log on and check out the pictures."

Doris begins to log on the iPad. While, Jonas whispered in Nia's ear.

"Nia, who hit Ken-Ken?"

"Jonas I think it was Shabazz." Jonas shook his head.

"I told you from the beginning to fuck that Board shit we're strong just, as B.O.G."

Doris glanced at both of them whispering, and knew it was serious.

"Listen, let me hit Shabazz, you know he's a problem anyway."

"Nah, we can't do that...We got to honor the treaty."

"Fuck that treaty, we protecting them niggas."

"Nia we can't go to war with the whole city."

"Listen, if we hit Shabazz no one would ever know who hit him...I know where his main bitch lives."

Jonas looked at her. "Yeah, I was dropping off some work on 77th and Greenwood, and he came rolling down the block. He never saw me...I'll wait on his ass, and hit him up."

"Nah, we need to find out, who did this first before we react."

Doris scrolled through the pictures, and tried not to be nosey. "Nia, where you was at?" asked Doris. Nia walked over, and looked on the screen.

"I was at the fight."

Jonas was on the other side of the bed looking at the pictures. He couldn't stop thinking about Ken-Ken's murder. Who would've disrespected his request? Jonas couldn't put his finger on it. The board seemed like they would let Blackout, handle Blackout affairs. But, Shabazz wouldn't let it go. Could it be him? Jonas knew Shabazz for years. Shabazz could be a hot head at times, but he disrespected the whole board, just to murder Ken-Ken. And do it so blatantly. Jonas couldn't put his finger on it, but Shabazz for the time- being as Nia's prime suspect.

"Listen, I got Trina waiting on me outside, so I'm going to bounce...I'll be back tomorrow."

Nia kissed Doris, and hugged Jonas.

"Make the call, and I'll deliver," whispered Nia as she was exiting the room.

"That girl is wild."

Doris just smiled. Knowing he was telling the truth.

Chapter 29

A ngela knew several days into the undercover investigation she compromised the entire investigation. There were strict rules and procedures when going undercover, but the charisma and charm of Jonas broke all those boundaries down.

As Angela made her way down Michigan Avenue, her mind was all over the place. What was supposed to be a simple investigation had turned into a love affair with one of Chicago's most ruthless gang leaders.

Angela phone beeped, and she looked down at the text which read, the results are back. Angela grabbed her phone, and immediately dialed a number.

"Doctor Taylor office, how may I help you."

"Doctor Taylor please..."

A series of clicks, and Dr. Taylor answered. "Dr. Taylor."

"Hi, Dr. Taylor this is Angela Becton I just received your text."

"Oh sure, hi Angela, let me pull up your chart, Please no, please no were all Angela thought. She didn't want it to be true. At least, not now.

"Okay here we go...All your blood work was fine, which is good."

"What about the pregnancy test?"

"Let me see." Dr. Taylor could be heard typing on the computer.

"Okay it's here...Angela you are six weeks pregnant."

Angela was speechless, as she held the phone staring into it. She never thought, her and Jonas would end up in bed, but after a long night out things got heated and before she knew what was going on, they both were naked getting it in without protection.

"Are you still there?"

"Yes, yes, what did you say?"

"You are six weeks pregnant."

Angela pulled over into a McDonalds parking lot, and tears begun to stream down her face. She couldn't believe. Angela's life at the agency was over. Career over.

"Thank you." Angela ended the call without even waiting to hear a response. What in the fuck do I do now were Angela thoughts, As she sat behind the Camry.

"Do I tell him or Do I have an abortion?" Angela mumbled. "This is to much."

Angela dialed a number, and after three rings someone answers.

"Hello"

"Hey Momma, how's things going?"

"Child, this little girl is all over the house"

Angela laughed. "She just finished doing my hair, got me looking all crazy."

Angela smiled. "All my blood work and stuff came back and it's good."

"Well, that's good."

"I had a pregnancy test done." Angela remained silent.

"And?"

"Well, Dr Taylor said I'm six weeks pregnant."

"I see somebody's been hot, hot huh?" Angela giggles.

"I don't know if I'm going to keep the baby."

"Child, if God blesses you with another child you don't have any right to take that life...you should have thought about that before you opened up your legs."

Angela had introduced Jonas to her mother, but she never told her, who Jonas really was or what he done for a living.

"I think Jonas would be a good father."

"Mom, I don't doubt that, but the whole situation is complicated."

"I got time. Tell me why it's so complicated...you told me you loved this man."

Angela came clean with her mother, and told her the entire story, and who Jonas really was and how he was the one she went undercover to bust. Her mother listened closely, as Angela went into details, and began to sob.

"Child, you don't have anything to sob about... sometimes love bites you in the ass."

"What do I do?"

"You call that boy up, and you be honest with him, and let him know you both need to talk."

"What about my job? I crossed the line."

"Do you like your job? I mean I prefer if you go back to nursing...that DEA thing is to dangerous...you see what happen to Michael."

Angela knew her mother was right. While, she liked being an agent she didn't like the boroughs bull shit working for the government. After Michael's death her heart was not into it like it was before. Not to mention she always thought about who would raise Nikki if she was killed in the line of duty. This alone caused her many sleepless nights.

"I can't tell him, I'm an agent."

"He going to find out one way or another."

"Listen, I'll come see you later." Angela ended the call and dialed another number.

"Hello."

"Hi Jonas."

Chapter 30

Bobby limped around the living room. Omar sat on the couch smoking a Newport. He had been held up in his condo since Diamond Dre's murder. Omar was tired of the beef. Money had been slow. Murder's Row had been, literally, shut down because of the murders. Omar started thinking about an exit plan.

"Did you think about the plan I had?" Omar asked. He wanted out of Chicago. At least until everything calmed down and got back to normal.

"What?"

"Seattle." Omar said.

Several months ago, Omar had tried to talk Bobby in to leaving for a little bit. It wasn't like they were running or nothing. Omar just wanted to leave. Joey had been murdered, and he didn't want to be next. Bobby didn't understand, though. He loved the drama. Nobody was going to be chasing him out of the city.

"Fuck Seattle!" Bobby plopped down on the sofa next to Omar. "Omar, I'm not going anywhere. I get them pussies on the ropes right now...You see what I did a couple days ago to that mutha fucka Ken-Ken!"

Omar saw the work on the television. It was a big thing. The Chicago Police had linked the whole incident to the

Blackout Gang, and had asked for the FBI's help in stemming the gang violence in the city. This made Omar even more determined to leave. He didn't want to risk getting caught up in the mix of a federal investigation with the B.O.G. It was pure stupid, especially when the Chief of Police sat on national television and cried for help.

"Look, Bobby I got a man out in Seattle that could set us up real good. We could go out there, set up another heroin spot, and make some money, quietly. At least until all these investigations go away, then we could come back stronger and kill Jonas and Nia."

"I was born in Chicago, and I'm dying in Chicago. They owe us a blood debt. My baby brother was killed, and through into the middle of the street like trash. The whole Chicago seen it or heard about it." Bobby shook his head, and calmed down. Every time he thought of Joey, he darn near came to tears. "And as for the investigations, fuck jail and those cops too because I'm not going back. I'm holding court right then and there. That's how I'm going."

Omar was convinced. Bobby still had the mentality of a street thug. No matter how much money he made, or power he gained over the years, Bobby wanted to still be on the front lines. Getting murder on the dirty streets of Chicago was his destiny, so he thought.

"Aye, Bobby-." Omar stopped to think clearly. "I'm leaving, and if you want to go with me your welcome. I already got a nice spot I rented waiting for me. Since you don't want to come I'm taking Joanna." Omar was hurt. He loved Bobby, but Bobby was always a bad decision maker. Bobby always thought with his ego, and let his arrogance make the wrong choices for him.

Chapter 31

From the moment Jonas heard Ken-Ken was hit things just didn't feel right. He had a lot of trust in the Board, and he couldn't see someone going behind his back and making such a bold move. But he knew if anybody would do so it was likely to be Shabazz.

Shabazz was somewhat of a living legend in the GO, and had a mean team of young gangsters from MOE town that would go to war with everybody. Moetown was a small area in Chicago from 53rd and Justine to 53rd and Loomis about a four block area. Shabazz built Moetown from the ground up when he left the federal penitentiary in the early 1990's.

Jonas knew Shabazz was loved in Moetown, and if the hit didn't go right, and B.O.G was implicated this would split the Board, and B.O.G would be fighting the entire city.

Jonas stood in the living room looking out the window. The city skyline came to life at night, and on a clear night it was truly beautiful.

Nia and Trina sat back on the sofa watching Jonas get his thoughts together. This was serious decision that had to be made. If it went wrong there would be problems for everybody.

"Trina, I need you to fly out to Chester, PA my main man Amir has a team out there...Bring them back to Chicago, so we could use them to hit Shabazz."

Amir was Jonas cellie in Joliet, and he ran Chester, PA with an iron fist. He had a team of young killers out in Chester PA, Killa Hill projects. Amir already told him the team was ready whenever he needed them, and now was the time.

Nia was shaking her head no. She didn't like the idea.

"Listen, we go outside the family with this one because in no way it can come back to us...I trust you Nia, but anything can go wrong."

"Yeah, I see your point, but I been doing this shit all my life, and if nothing else I know how to hit a motherfucker."

"Nia, he knows that, I know that, shit the whole city know, but I like Jonas's thinking on this one."

Nia gave Trina a dirty look.

"Trina, you go up there to Chester, and give Nieem a rundown on the hit...Bring him and his team back to the Go...Nia when they get here you take them on a few dry runs so they get familiar with the area, and we sit back and wait."

"I'm with you."

"Good, now when the hit goes down get them out the city fast...I'll make sure we have a private flight ready to go ASAP."

Nia begin to smile.

"Why you smiling?"

She didn't have a reason, other than the fact that, she was just happy Jonas was going after Shabazz.

"No reason. Let's just get this thing on the move."

Chapter 32

Trina landed at Philadelphia International Airport on a red eye flight from Chicago. The flight was short and quick. She managed to relax for the first time in months. The war with the Bogus Boyz had kept her on high alert, day and night.

She strolled out of the terminal carrying a hand bag filled with mostly hygiene material. Toothbrush, soap, deodorant, make up and a few fragrances. Trina looked shinning. She had heard a lot about the big city of Philadelphia, but not a lot about her designated visit of Chester, PA, a small city that was ten minutes away tucked between Delaware and Philly. The weather was still nice, and just right for Trina's tight, army green, dress skirt by BCBG. She wore a pair of nude colored pumps by Gucci to go along with the outfit. The skirt was strapless, and covered her medium-sized melons, and came half way up her thigh.

Trina rode the escalator down to the bottom level, and stepped over to the baggage claim area. She waited for a couple seconds, then her Louis Vuitton designed, suit case slowly came past on the rubber motorized bed. Trina grabbed the one piece of luggage. She had only planned on spending one night in Chester. It was gather the boys up, and be on the next flight back with them to Chicago. Business had to be taken care of, and quickly. Trina strutted through the double glassed doors, and waited for her ride.

A black BMW 760i pulled up, and stopped a few feet from where Trina was standing. Cabs, shuttle busses and people crowded the area. Trina noticed the car, but didn't think nothing of it. The person that Jonas had described to her was extremely low-key, and drove regular trucks and cars but nothing as expensive and foreign, as the black European that pulled up to the curb.

A brown skin man stepped out of the car. He had a thick beard, and very low hair cut. Although, he use to wear it in a little blow out and faded in the back, and by the ears. He wore a navy blue Polo shirt with the big red horse on the front, in the left corner. Along with semi-faded denim jeans, and a pair of tan construction Tim's.

He stared at the red bone with her long black hair in a pony tail. He moved straight over to her. Trina smiled and then caught herself. "What's up? Trina, right?" he asked skeptical.

"Yeah."

"My name's Nieem." He said and then extended his hand towards her. She grabbed it and gave him a light hand shake.

"Yeah, Amir's my people's."

"Yeah, I heard a lot about him, and you."

"Oh did you! I hope everything was good."

"For sure."

"You ready?" Nieem asked, then without a response he grabbed her luggage, and walked towards his car. He popped the trunk, and placed the single suitcase inside, then moved over to the driver's side door. Trina waited, and sized him up. She loved his swag. Trina stared uncontrollable, and visualized how the short man could be so dangerous, and look so sexy too.

"The door is unlocked." Nieem said, and smiled before getting in the car.

Trina smiled to herself, and felt embarrassed that he caught her lusting off him.

Nieem sped off, and headed straight for the highway. He made it to the ramp. They took I95 south, and headed straight for Chester, The traffic was crowded, and slow. Due to the fact it was after four in the afternoon, and a lot of workers were just getting off of work. They rode in silence for a bit. Both had seemed to shy in order to spark a conversation.

"So you from Chicago, huh?"

"Yeah."

"How is it down there? I've never been there before."

"It's all good. It ain't any different from any other cities, except of course we got a heavy gang culture, which I heard y'all don't around here."

"Nah, we don't have none of that. Mostly neighborhoods or streets going hard together, but nothing organized or with rules and shit like Jonas and them. You on that Blackout squad right?"

She nodded her head, yes. Trina crossed her legs trying to show a little bit of thighs, and to see if he was checking her out like she was scoping him out. Nieem's eyes glanced straight down her smooth legs, then up to her melons wrapped tightly in the dress.

The traffic had cleared up a little, once he made it past the Ridley township exit. Nieem hit the gas, and made it down to the Highland Avenue exit within five minutes. He came to the stop sign, and made a right. Nieem went over a little hill, then sped down through the green light. For some reason, he was in a rush. Trina slouched back in the tan leather seats, but still remained focus. She studied her new environment, and paid attention to all the land marks. Once past the light, Nieem made a left into a residential neighborhood.

Highland Gardens was the name, but Killa Hill is what it was known by. The neighborhood was notorious for its killings, drugs and broad daylight shoot-outs. Two major Federal indictments over the past ten years emerged from the area. One involving Nieem, and his crew called the Young Gunz. They had been indicted for Tampering with a witness by murder, racketeering offenses and violating the federal drug laws. Nieem managed to get his case dismissed before trial with the help of a family member named Lil Nigga, and the rest of his co-defendants got convicted, and was sentenced to life without the possibility of parole. The other indictment came from a spot called the Circle of Death. The two groups was only separated by two blocks, but both had managed to make a lot of money in the small neighborhood.

Nieem, now had the whole place to himself including an apartment complex and several out-of-town customers, who he served weekly. After getting indicted and returning home, Nieem came back around his old stomping grounds. The city had tore down half of the neighborhood trying to clean it up. They claimed the homes were old, and ran down, and they needed to be fixed and updated to comply with the modern day quality of living. The place was old, but they really were sending a message that, they weren't tolerating no more drug activity on his old block, Boyle street. He understood the silent threat, and moved his operation around the back of the neighborhood. Park Terrace to be exact. It really consisted of an apartment complex, but everybody always considered it apart of Killa Hill. Nieem went, and set up shop. He had a team of youngsters selling weed, and powder cocaine. The place on a good day brought in twenty thousand, and that was strictly from powder sells. The marijuana alone averaged around ten-to-fifteen thousand a day too. And Nieem controlled it all, mostly with family members and lifelong friends from the neighborhood.

Nieem reached under the seat, and grabbed a Ruger, forty-five additions. He laid it on Trina's lap, and told her to hold on to it for him.

During their short conversation, Nieem had managed to explain to Trina the beef he had with a group of snitches called, By All Means. They had been going at it for awhile, and he let her know it wouldn't be over to either, he was killed, or their leader Shitty was killed. Shitty was a snitch, which killed Nieem's uncle, Saleem. Niee didn't bore her with the in-depth story, but he just gave her enough so that she could be vigilant when she was with him.

Two youngsters, no older that fifteen, sat on the metal gate that surrounded the corner home. It stood a few feet from the stop sign. They were smoking weed, and looking ruff on the sunny day. They both wore denim jeans, and black long-sleeved shirts that looked like they had slept with them on, and wore them all week.

Nieem rode past the deserted street where the Circle of Death had amassed their wealth, then sent to prison with long sentences. The place was in disarray, and children played on the small filty street. Nieem slow rolled to the stop sign. Trina stared over at the two dirty looking kids. She grabbed the gun, and held it tightly. It was heavy and black. The P90 did damage. It held eight hollow tip bullets, and had one already in the chamber. She trained her eyes on them. She was a murderer, and knew that you couldn't underestimate anybody, whether they were eleven or sixty-two years old. Nieem saw the glare in her eye.

The two youngsters leaped off the gate at the site of Nieem's BMW pulling up. Trina's finger shadowed the trigger, as she lifted it up to aim at the two kids. At the sight of the gun, they paused. Nieem leaned over, and tapped her arm down. "Hold up, little momma!" He beeped the horn twice, and they raised their hands, and gave a nod with it, in order to say what's up.

"They with me."

"Oh!" Trina said, placing the gun back on her waist.

Nieem just smiled at her. He liked her style. Pretty, and ready for whatever. He made a mental note of that and then made a left on Culhane Street. Nieem rode around to the apartment complex. Unlike when they entered the neighborhood, Park terrace was packed. Kids, junkies, hustlers, and females sat around in front of the complexes, some in front of their own place and some in front of others. The place was drug infested, and looked exactly like it too. Some places were abandoned; others had broken windows with trash bags covering it from the outside conditions, while others were barely livable.

Trina had recognized the place when she seen it. The complex was just like any other drug spot, except it looked like they really thought it was legal to sell the drugs. The young hustlers openly sold cocaine to whites, and blacks pulling up in cars, as well as them walking up on foot.

Nieem pulled over to the curb behind a rundown truck. He looked over to Trina. "We only going to be here for a second. My two young bulls that are going to do the job are right over there waiting for me." Nieem pointed over to a crowd of people. They sat in lawn chairs, while some stood up. All of them were smoking, either weed or Newport's.

"I'm straight playboy. Just make sure you keep me safe." She said, trying to sound sexy, then smiled at the remark herself.

"Oh, you got my word, not a single piece of hair on you is going to be harmed...I got other plans for you." He got out of the car before she could respond back.

Trina sat in the car smiling at nobody, but herself. She was feeling him, but playing shy, and hard to get. Not tonight, though. Trina thought, She planned on making this trip memorable. She was out of town, and to top it off she haven't had none in months. Trina was horny, and giving it up to an out-of-towner was the perfect excitement she needed in her sex life, especially to a smooth brother like Nieem.

He strolled over, and dapped up everybody on the side of the building. Then he pulled two youngsters to the side, and began talking to them.

Chapter 33

Nieem lay across the queen size bed wrapped in sheets. He was naked underneath and perspiring lightly. He was awake, but o the verge of going back to sleep. Nieem just got finished having wild sex with the light skin beauty next to him. He needed sleep, though. He had a big day ahead of him.

Trina sat on the edge of the bed. She was completely naked, except for the white sheet covering her lower body, stopping right underneath her navel. After, the late night love making lasting all the way until the early morning, something was bothering her. It wasn't the man lying in the bed next to her. For the past week, the two had been inseparable. Trina brought Nieem, and his two young boys, back to Chicago. She showed them around the city, and took them through all the precautions and necessary places that they needed to know in order to make their trip successful. Now, they were just waiting for the order. Jonas had been procrastinating. He wanted to make sure it was truly Shabazz, who got Ken-Ken killed.

The room was dark except for the moon light shining through the huge window, bringing out the tan carpet. The shades had been drawn all night, and Chicago's city lights glared in the background. Trina had rented the suite for the week, in order to be underneath Nieem before he left the city after taking care of Shabazz. It had been awhile since she caught real feelings over a man. She had sex, as often as she felt like, but that wasn't all she thought about. Trina wanted a man in her life, but not from Chicago. She had killed too many men and women in the city to just fall in love with a man from there. So, she guarded her feelings extremely close.

Nieem sat up, and leaned his back on the glass head board.

"What's up shorty you ain't?"

"I'm good. I just was thinking about this thing that happened awhile back."

"What happen?"

"It's nothing. Don't worry I'm okay." She said, then turned around to look at him. "Go ahead to sleep. We been up all night." She smiled. "I hope ya youngbull's...Ain't that how y'all say it?"

Nieem nodded, yes.

"I hope they didn't hear us in here." Trina was embarrassed that she had let herself go in the midst of their love making. She would usually be reserved with one of her young lovers, but Nieem was different.

"They over there with two young girls, so they pretty much occupied."

"You right. Go ahead to sleep, though. I'm going to lay down in a minute."

The murder of Ken-Ken kept bothering her. Not the fact that he was murdered, but who the masked man was. She saw him when he got out of the van with a limp, but didn't pay it no mind, at the time. Ever since returning back to Chicago, she had been replaying the scene back in her head. Not on her own though. Jonas had been the one, who brought this about. He kept questioning her and Nia about the person. Jonas wanted to be sure. The Board was looking good. Gang related murders dropped since the treaty, except for minor in-house fighting amongst each other in their particular gangs. Money was being made, and the coming winter looked like it was going to be a good year for the B.O.G.

Trina concentrated harder, the limp kept giving her the problem. She knew most of Shabazz's hitters, and top level members. None walked with a limp, or bop, or any other defect that could've been pin-pointed to them. Maybe Nia overreacted, and blamed Shabazz to soon. That was the thought on Trina's mind.

She stood up, still with the sheet wrapped around her bottom half. Nieem rolled over, and pulled the white comforter over him. Trina moved over by the window. Her reddish-brown nipples were poked out, due to the chill in the room, she didn't feel the air, though. "Fuck!" She mumbled. Trina dropped the sheet, and raced over to the nightstand to her phone. Nieem rolled over and glared at her. Trina's nude body casted a silhouette in the room from the moon's light. Nieem admired her curves, and toned shape in the dark.

"What's up?"

"Nothing! Something just hit me. I got to call Nia right quick." She snatched the phone up, yelled her name in the phone. The phone automatically picked up her voice request, and Nia's phone started ringing.

Nia had been sick for the past week, or so. Morning sickness, mood swings, and a lack of appetite. She had been staying at Jonas's condo while Angela took care of her. Nia was fine except for the fever, one-time, but everything else was due to her having a baby. Jonas had tried to convince her to leave the city, and head home to Vegas. She declined. Nia wasn't leaving until she killed Bobby, and that was that.

Trina tried three more times, but still no answer. She disconnected the line, and start putting her close on. Nieem reached over to the nightstand, and turned the light on. Trina was fully dressed by now. She had on her tight Chanel jeans, colorful Polo boots for women, and white long sleeve, Prada cotton dress shirt.

"Where you going at?" He looked over at the clock. "It's 5:30 in the morning."

"I got to make a run real fast, don't worry I'll be back. I just got to take care of something." She walked over, and kissed Nieem on the lips. Then reached under the pillow for her forty caliber Sith and Wesson. "If, I don't be back by tonight, you got everybody numbers, but tell Jonas to hold off on Shabazz until I get back."

"Why? Ain't that why I came down here to hit the bull?"

"Yeah, but just trust me. Tell him what I said. I'll be back baby. Love you." Trina stunned herself when she said it, but kept moving. She meant it, but didn't know it for certain.

Nieem didn't respond. He had two wives back in Chester. He was Muslim, so under his Islamic teachings it was permissible to have two wives. But not have unprotected, and adulterous sex with a non-believing woman like Trina. That was against everything the religion stood for, but Nieem also killed people, and sold drugs. He was living wrong anyway. Trina wouldn't understand any of it, though, and he knew it was going to be hard breaking off their sudden relationship. He had too.

Bobby limped out of the Riverview glass doors. Cindy followed him, and held her daughter, Tasha's hand tightly. Ever since Cindy showed that she was a little rida, Bobby been showing her love. She was just one of his many women, but Cindy was the youngest at twenty-three. So, he tried to show her a little bit more love, if you called banging her twice a week, then spending money on her. Cindy didn't mind. Her baby father was dead. She struggled financially trying to take care of Tasha, so the harsh treatment dished out by Bobby didn't matter. She dealt with worst men, at times throughout her young life.

Cindy moved the long micro-braids out of her face and then picked up the brown skin three year old, so she could carry her to the car. Tasha was walking to slow. They both were dressed in black jeans, and leather jackets. Bobby had bought the girls almost identical Gucci jackets except Tasha had a Gucci for kid's version.

The stars had just disappearing, but the sky was still dark. It was a little chilly on the October morning. Bobby loved this hour of the day, though. Everybody was still sleeping, in bed from the partying the night before. This was his time to conduct business. He went, and opened the Murder's Row, hunted down some leads on Jonas, Nia, or other members of the Blackout and then when daylight arrived; he was back in Omar's condo. He stayed in with a female until the night feels again. Bobby had his routine down pack since he came home from the hospital.

Omar had already left for Seattle with Joanna, so Bobby kept the spot. And, he enjoyed it too. No more nagging Omar to second guess his decisions. Even though he wasn't putting in no work anyway.

Bobby held the door open for Cindy. It was his habit to let her walk out first in case anybody was waiting to hit him outside. She would be his shield. It was disturbing, but Bobby was a survivor. By all means, he wasn't getting shot again.

He wore a grey Polo sweat suit with the hood attached, black Nike boots, and a black, Pell Pell, leather jacket. Cindy headed straight for her Ford Taurus, parked o the main street in front of the building. Bobby followed, but scanned the scene. He was looking for any unusual cars or trucks parked around the vicinity. Bobby strolled, with his slight limp, and spotted a SUV with a person lying low inside if it...He didn't break his stride, though, he caught up with Cindy. "Aye, go ahead, and warm the car up. I got to grab something, but be on point. Don't look back, but it's a navy blue Explorer back there with somebody in it." Cindy didn't need to be explained the rest she been with Bobby for a couple months now, and knew what he was on. Cindy was just mad that Tasha was with her.

Bobby went and acted like he was going to get in the car, then stopped and he strolled back over to the building's entrance, then went inside...Bobby stayed strap. He headed straight for the back of the building. Bobby glanced at his watch. It read 6:00am. The sun wouldn't rise for another hour at least. He speed walked, with his limp, out the backdoor. Bobby's brain started to race. Who could it be? Police. Fed's.

Nia and Trina. He didn't know. Nobody knew he lived at the place, but everybody knew Omar lived there.

He darted out into the darkness of the early morning. Bobby crept up on the sidewalk. He kept his eyes alert, and hands in his jacket pocket on the gun. Bobby was carrying a 9mm today. He carried it just to get around the city. He didn't need nothing bigger, unless he was on a mission. Bobby moved swiftly past a car, and a truck. The Ford Explorer sat in front of a caravan. Bobby eased up on the rear of the explorer. He glared inside, quickly, then moved towards the passenger door. Bobby raised the gun first and then yanked the door open.

She just stared at him. No fear showed in her demeanor.

"Put ya hands on the wheel, bitch!"

She complied with the order. Trina had been caught slipping. Damn! She thought to herself. Trina had been, so caught up with the fact that Bobby was the one, who killed Ken-Ken, she was off point. She failed to watch her surroundings. This was a first for her, and maybe the last.

A forty caliber lay on the passenger seat. "Oh, you was about to hit me with this here, huh!" Bobby said, while grabbing the gun, and getting in the Explorer. He kept the gun on her, and hit the horn twice. Cindy looked over. Bobby waved her over with the gun. She knew what time it was. This hadn't been the first time Bobby thought somebody was parked on the street looking for him, so he made sure Cindy knew the drill. Cindy turned around, and pulled along side of the Explorer.

Bobby looked around the vehicle. He needed to tie her hands with something. He couldn't find anything. Trina had seen the look in his eyes. She knew he didn't want to kill there, so she was going to try him.

"Keep ya hands on the wheel, bitch!" yelled Bobby.

"Bobby you ain't going to kill me here."

He didn't hesitate like she thought. Bobby participated in to many kidnappings, murders, and robberies. He knew to never let the victim sense any weakness. Bobby smacked her across the face with the pistol. Trina's pretty faced, immediately, starts leaking, and turned red. The blow dazed her, but she was still conscious.

Cindy double-parked in the street, and threw the hazards on. She jumped out of the car with an orange, silk, Hermes scarf that had been lying on the passenger seat. She went straight to the driver's door, looked inside, and seen the bloody woman. Bobby waved her in. She opened the door.

"Tie her hands." He ordered.

Cindy did, as told. She quickly tied both hands up with the long scarf, tight.

"Hurry up, and open the trunk. We taking the bitch with us."

Cindy just looked at him, like he was crazy or something. She wanted to say no, but couldn't. They had murdered a man together already. Cindy was locked in with the crazy man, now. She had to do it. Regardless, if Tasha was in the car with them or not, she hated herself for being in this predicament. Cindy stormed off, but left the door open.

The bloody Trina saw the opportunity. This was her last shot at making it out alive, or getting a bullet dying. She leaped out of the open door.

"Shit!" Bobby aimed at her, but didn't shoot. He stormed out of the passenger side door.

Cindy saw her try to escape. She threw the car in reverse, and bumped Trina. The truck door flew open. Trina fell hard to the ground, spraining her ankle. Bobby pounced on Trina, and griped her up, then threw her in the trunk.

Trina had moved to soon. She lay curled up in the dark trunk, thinking. She knew Bobby had been the one when she seen him limping out of the buildings. Although, she was suprised to see him, she was ready. So, she thought.

Trina had just camped outside of Omar's building to follow him. Maybe he would lead her to Bobby? Trina never thought that Bobby would walk out of the building six o' clock in the morning.

Her brain raced, and ached from the blow. Blood continued to flow. Trina had a big gash, over top of her eye that needed stitches to fix, but she wasn't getting any help. Or, was just going to relay the information to Jonas, and them. Bobby was the culprit, not Shabazz. She struggled at the scarf again. Her hands were sore and starting to get numb. Trina kicked the side of the car. She was determined to get out of the trunk. Even, if it meant losing both her hands in the process.

Chapter 34

T he whole crew scoured the city looking for Trina. Jonas called her phone, every fifteen minutes, trying to see if she was alright, and what information she had. Trina had been missing since 5:30 in the morning.

Nieem had woken up, around 8:30, and called Jonas. He explained everything Trina had said, then got dressed and went to the next room to chill with his two young goons.

Jonas called everybody. Nobody seemed to have seen her. He reached out to Nakira, and told her to check around the different precincts to see if she got locked up. But, by six o'clock that night nothing turned up. Jonas still planned on waiting for the move.

Nia was sick, on this particular day, so she wasn't of no help. She tried several times to get out of the bed and go looking for her partner. Angela wouldn't let her. Nia was weak, feeling bloated, and had a slight temperature.

Shabazz drove down 79th street in his dark green Infinity truck. He made a left on Greenwood, right under the railroad tracks, and sped down the two-lane street. Shabazz was checking his stomping grounds out. Ever since the treaty, and became a member of the Board, money been flowing through Moetown. He hooked up with Trina, and she was showing love on the prices. Shabazz didn't have no complaints except that Ken-Ken issue. He was happy when he got murdered, but didn't like how Jonas handled. Ken-Ken was a rat. So, anybody should've been able to kill him on sight.

He slowed up at the stop sign. A crowd of men stood, under a lamp post, in front of a ran down home. Shabazz didn't stop. He wasn't looking for anyone in particular, just riding through after picking up some money from a few streets over.

Shabazz sped past the group of men, and sped, faster, down the street. He went through a stop sign, without stopping, and a sky blue Crown Victorian pulled in back of him. A flashing, police, light immediately started bouncing off the homes. The lights sat right on the dash board of the Crown Vic.

"Shit!" Shabazz mumbled. He slowed down, hoping the cop wouldn't pull him over.

The Crown Victorian was directly in back of the truck. The lights were flashing, bright in the darkness of the night, but no sounds of the regular noise came from the car.

Shabazz stopped in the middle of the street. It was dark, and no street lights occupied this particular area of the street. Cars and trucks lined both sides of Greenwood, so there was nowhere to pull over, and park. He threw the truck in park, and practiced his speak before the cop approached.

The man exited the cruiser. He had on a black suite, white shirt, rubber sole shoes, and black Fedora pulled tight on his head. He looked nice, and professional. His beard was husky, and he had a brown skin complex. He approached Shabazz's window.

His window slide down. "What did I do wrong, Detective?" He had figured that the man was a Detective. Shabazz never seen him around there before, or was he driving in a regular marked vehicle.

"You ran that stop sign back there, sir. Do you have you license, and registration?"

Shabazz was stuck. He didn't have either on him. Shabazz gazed over, and looked at the book bag, filled with money on the floor. He taking it. Damn!

"No, but-"

"Could you please step out of the truck, Mr." The Detective reached for his firearm, hanging on the right side of his waist in the hoister. "It smells like marijuana in the truck also. Were you smoking?"

Shabazz had just finished smoking a Dutch before he hit 79th street. He complied with the order, and stepped out the vehicle. The man placed Shabazz on the side of the Infinity to check him. The lights bounced off the residential homes.

"Place your hands on top of the vehicle. Do you have any firearms on you?"

A car pulled up in back of the Crown Victorian and then pulled alongside of the Infinity. The man turned to look, but before he could say anything, two youngsters - seventeen years old, leaped out of the red Grand Am. Farad's firearm was raised high in the air. He wore a black Dickie, Zip-up, hoodie, denim jeans and black Timberlands; quarter length cut. His dark skin complexion, and brown eyes gazed upon Shabazz with his hands stretched, and legs sprawled open across the truck. He waved Nieem back to the Crown Victorian.

Tyson appeared right on the side of Furad. He wore the same thing, all the way down to the boots except he was brown skin, and held a silver colt .45, army addition.

Shabazz was confused. He seen the Grand Am pull up, but thought it was the Task Force. They had similar cars, but why would them, and Detective be pulling him over. He couldn't figure it out.

Tyson fired first. Boom! The first shot caught Shabazz in the left shoulder. "Where the money at? Where the money at?"

Shabazz was still standing. Farad didn't wait for a reply. He let off a barrage of bullets. Tyson followed suit. Shabazz was catching bullets in the back, legs, buttock, and a few head shots. They emptied their clips. Shabazz fell directly back. His head hit the ground with a small thud sound. Tyson jumped over him, and went into the truck. Farad stayed put, eyeing the neighborhood for any unwanted guest. Police, neighborhoods, or any BPS gang member, who had been posted up several blocks away.

Nieem stayed behind the wheel of the Crown Victorian. He held a police scanner in his hand.

Tyson stormed out of the truck with a book bag. He raced around to the passenger side. Farad jumped in the driver seat, and waited for Tyson to get in finally. He raced off down the street, and Nieem followed.

The truck door was left open, and Shabazz lay in a puddle of his own blood, a few feet away. His whole back, riddled with bullets. Shabazz was dead.

Neighbors started coming out, BPS gang members from up the street had ran down to the scene, after the shooting was done, to see what happened. The crowd surrounded him. Shabazz was well-known in the area, a legend of some sort. There he lay. A legend had fallen and none of his soldiers, helpers, or followers were there to help save him.

Nieem had been tailing Shabazz for the past hour. He had taken turns with Ford following him in the Grand Am, but Shabazz failed to notice them, if he had maybe the outcome would've been different.

Jonas had made it clear before they left that, if Shabazz didn't go to his stash house, and pick up some money then he didn't want him touched. He needed it to look like a robbery, and a robbery-homicide it was.

Trina lie hog-tied, naked, and the top of Hustler's Row. Chicago PD had just arrived, after the call, and started closing the area off.

The blood was fresh, and still leaking. It was 12:30 at night. Bobby had dropped Trina off five minutes in the same Ford Explorer she tried to lie on him in. The murder was symbolic. A message, he was sending to Jonas. Bobby was revenging his brother's death, Joey. They had killed Joey the same way, and threw his body on Murder's Row like a piece of trash. Now, Trina was being treated the same way.

Chapter 35

The room was peacefully quiet, and dark. A television hung up on the wall, and flashes from the screen brought forth much needed light, here and there. Doris was in the bed. Her face was sunken in, skin had lighted up considerably, and her head was completely bald now, but it was covered by a black long wig. Angela had brought it for her a week ago. The wig had brightened her spirits up a bit, but Doris knew she was on the verge of dying. The pain was getting worse, other organs in her body started to becoming a problem, and her kidney was failing by the day. She didn't want to fight no more. The world and all its problems were behind Doris, now. She thought about her two kids, Jonas and Nia, and wished the best for them, then Doris took her last breath.

Flip Toney had informed Jonas about Trina's murder. Jonas raced down to Hustler's Row. He got there, and Trina was still lying in the street. Nothing covered her. The whole neighborhood witnessed Trina's ravaged body. Jonas looked at her with sadness in his heart. He tried to get the cops, who had the scene taped off with yellow tape, to cover her up with some sheets. They wouldn't do it, though. They had got specific orders from their Chief to leave her, as is. Chicago PD wanted to do a thorough investigation of Trina's murder, and wanted to show other gang members and neighborhoods how serious the violence had got over the years. The Chief was trying to take a stand against the city of over hundred thousand or more gang members. The Mayor, Governor, and State Representatives were coming down hard on the Chief, and police department for their lack of ability to step the gang violence.

Jonas stayed on the scene for awhile, then left. He had to go make sure Nieem and his boys got out of town safely. They did. Jonas placed Nieem, Farad, and Tyson on a train headed for Chester, Pennsylvania. This had been Nieem's request. He didn't want to fly back home. Nieem always loved to play it safe. The train had arrived at three in the morning and Jonas stayed with her until the end.

Jonas had made a few calls, while he was there to Mark, Nakira, and Flip. He was making arrangements for Nia to leave in the morning on the first flight to Las Vegas. Jonas wasn't asking her, he was telling her, she was leaving for awhile. With Trina's death, and funeral coming, and Bobby still roaming the streets, Jonas didn't want the unwanted stress on Nia. It would be too hard for her, and the baby. She already had a nervous breakdown, and was threatening to murder everybody associated with Bobby Mackey, when she got the news. Nia was on the verge of losing her baby. Angela helped by comforting her, and calming Nia down. Trina murder was hard on Nia. After Jonas made all the arrangements with Mark, he got Angela to pack Nia's things up, and take her to the airport.

He was drained from all the news, and other activities. Jonas arrived home at 5:30am. Angela and Nia had left the condo hours ago. He dove on the sofa head first, and fell to sleep. Jonas, still had his clothes on, and didn't even bother to take his sneakers off, either.

Boom! Four en wearing all black bullet-proof vests, with DEA SWAT in yellow going across the front, dash thru the door. They carried assault rifles, with flash lights attached to the top of them, aimed at different directions of the condo. Roger Freeman follows them in the condo. He has a double-pump shot gun in his hand. Roger dressed in a hooded, grey, sweat shirt, bullet-proof vest over the top of his sweatshirt, and denim jeans.

Jonas leaped up at the sound. He was confused. Jonas doesn't know who the people were running threw his condo at this time of hour.

"Hands in the air! Hands in the air!" Roger said. He was the first one to spot Jonas on the sofa. Jonas complied, and raised his hands high in the air.

The raids had been successful, and netted forty-eight gang members. The DEA's drug task force, along with Chicago's gang task force, raided several homes of Blackout gang members. Flip Toney was arrested without resistance. He had been caught at home with two million dollars in cash hidden inside a washing machine. The money was carefully placed in the bottom secret compartment that nobody knew about except him and the maker.

Nakira's house and sister's home were raided, and searched thoroughly by the gang unit. The Night Stalker personally arrested her, and had a vicious smile on his face when he placed the cuffs on her. They considered Nakira rouge cop. She went against her oath, shield, and everything the Chicago Police stood for. Dignity, Integrity, and Honor. The gang unit was a special section, and the officers were carefully handpicked. The Night Stalker, Chief of Police, and the Mayor was embarrassed and ashamed to have one of their own, working with the same criminals that they were trying to get off the streets. They wanted to make an example out of Nakira.

Nakira understood the treatment. She held her head high when they escorted her to an awaiting squad car to be taking her away.

Chapter 36

The noise was loud, and obnoxious. B.O.G's younger member's barked insults and offensive language at every United States Marshal that walked past the metal cage. There were ten of them in each of the five dingy cages.

Jonas and Flip Toney sat by each other near the open bars. They both were tired, frustrated, and confused on how they had been indicted. The whole thing was a mystery. Both of them had insulated their selves, so deep in the chain of command that it would've been nearly impossible to get any type of incriminating evidence on them, especially with the help of Nakira. She was an old love, friend, and biggest supporter.

Two marshals stepped in front of the cell. One of the young members moved closer to the cage to give them a piece of his mind, or even spit on them.

All the noise and aggressive behavior was getting on Jonas's nerves. He needed to think, and think quickly.

"Aye D-Roc! Calm down Joe. Let me hear what they got to say."

D-Roc nodded, and moved towards the back of the filthy cell.

"Paul Jonas and Darrnell Toney come on, so y'all can get arraigned."

Jonas and Flip stepped up to the gate. The two got cuffed and were taking up to see the Magistrate Judge.

The Court Room was crowded, and now only provided for observes to stand in the back of the room. Jonas strolled into the room, and scanned the place. Flip was directly behind him. Jonas was searching for Angela, nobody else. She was nowhere to be found. He kept looking though. Jonas locked eyes with a teary eyed Lisa. She blew him a kiss, and whispered I love you. Tia clung to her mother's leg. The pretty little girl face was emotionless. Tia looked at her dad, and then put her head down.

He was crushed by her action. Jonas had promised her that he would never return back to prison, no matter what.

The Night Stalker, Special Agent Roger Freeman, and James Weinstein stood behind a wooden table. All of them had a grin of happiness on their faces, as Flip Toney and Jonas walked passed them to be placed in front of the Judge's desk.

With the killing of Ken-Ken, the Night Stalker suspected that there was a leak within his unit. Nobody had known about Ken-Ken cooperation except several few, and Nakira had been one of them. The Night Stalker went out and sought help from Agent Roger Freeman. They still had a witness, Marcus, willing to testify, and he would point the finger at Jonas and Flip, as his supplier of the forty-six kilo's. James Weinstein had convinced him to do it. He did first to get promoted to the federal district attorney's office, and second to help his friend, The Night Stalker out on getting his first federal conviction. Roger had agreed to help, and placed Nakira under surveillance. He didn't get any hard core evidence on her, but he got some circumstantial stuff. Like Jonas calling her, and visiting her, nothing that she should've been indicted for. They didn't care though. The three veterans were banking on her cooperating, or some others, then they would build a more solid case on the B.O.G.

Flip and Jonas stepped up to the front of the tall mahogany bench of Judge Wolf. Jonas remained distracted by his daughter's reaction. Tia and Lisa were running through his mind. He had let her down once again.

The door opened in the back, where Jonas and Flip had just entered through. Everybody focused their attention on the woman walking up being escorted by a US Marshal. Nakira was shackled from the front, and placed directly on the left side of Jonas.

Jonas couldn't comprehend why. Nakira in cuffs? He was flabbergasted. Nakira had never took part in B.O.G's activities, in anyway. At least nobody knew of it. Jonas shook his hand at her. He leaned over, and whispered. "I'm sorry."

She nodded her head, and then leaned over to him. "I'm sorry Jonas, Agent Freeman just told me Doris died this morning." Nakira didn't get to finish the rest of her statement on how Roger tried to get her to cooperate against Jonas.

Jonas dripped his head. Pain shot through his body like a lightning bolt. This was the biggest blow that the world could've sent his way. Doris meant everything to Jonas. The pressure became even harder for him, at the very moment. He composed himself though.

"Now, this is case number 13-00162." Judge Wolf shuffled some papers, then glared down on the three defendants. "Since all three of you's are alleged, charged with the same conspiracy I'm going to read it out together, and for the record this pertains to all three defendants until I say otherwise."

The Judge waited for any objections by the defendants. They raised none. Everybody was trapped in their own worlds at the time. "In Count One of the indictment the government alleges that Paul Jonas and Darrell Toney each controlled five or more persons with the intent to distribute cocaine, cocaine base, and heroin in violation of 21 U.S.C. 848 (a) and (b), which is running a Continuing criminal enterprise." The Judge peered down again and then continued. "Count two of the indictment the government alleges that Paul Jonas, Nakira Whitehurst and other unknown conspirators to the grand jury, Tampered with a witness by murder in the death of Denneth Peace, In violation of the Federal Statute 18 U.S.C. 1512 (a) (I) (A), which carried the penalty of death."

Nakira remained cool, but was shocked at the charge: the death penalty for the murder of Ken-Ken. His heart skipped a beat, and started racing all at once. She stared at Jonas for comfort, but he was lost. He didn't recover from the news of Doris's death, so the rest of the charges were nothing more than a blur to him.

Angela stepped into the room she looked fantastic dressed in a black pant suite and heels, but was beat on the inside. She had got word from the hospital of Doris death, and been notified by Roger of Jonas's arrest. Angela felt like a traitor, piece of shit, and outright Judas. Jonas had entrusted her to be around his family, and friends. She came to the conclusion that it was over. she was keeping the baby, and resigning from the agency, but still wanted to be in Jonas life.

Roger stood at the window, overlooking the city. Angela didn't bother to knock, or anything before she entered his office.

"Roger!"

He turned around and then folded his arms across his chest. Roger still had a grin on his face from the victory of taking down Jonas. Even though, he missed his intended target, Nia.

"How are you doing, Angela?"

"I'm fine. I'm just have to let you know that I'm resigning, I'll have my resignation papers on your desk by the end of the business day."

"Are you still willing to testify against Jonas?"

"No, because I didn't get anything incriminating against him."

Roger stared at her. "You sure?"

"Yes."

"I'll be waiting for the resignation papers then."

Angela turned to leave, but was stopped in her tracks by Roger clearing his throat.

"I talked to the doctor, and I know about your relationship with him."

Angela's heart dropped at the mention of the doctor. She didn't know what to say next.

"It's alright! This one is on me." Roger said.

Proof

Made in the USA
Charleston, SC
28 May 2014